T0067991

Database Management for Business Leaders

Building and Using Data Solutions
That Work for You

LARRY RUDDELL

WESTBOW
P R E S S®
A DIVISION OF THOMAS NELSON
& ZONDERVAN

WestBow Press books may be ordered through booksellers or by contacting:

WestBow Press
A Division of Thomas Nelson & Zondervan
1663 Liberty Drive
Bloomington, IN 47403
www.westbowpress.com
844-714-3454

ISBN: 978-1-9736-3024-1 (sc)
ISBN: 978-1-9736-3026-5 (hc)
ISBN: 978-1-9736-3025-8 (e)

Library of Congress Control Number: 2018906931

Print information available on the last page.

WestBow Press rev. date: 6/29/2018

To my friends and colleagues in the information technology world; Bob, Jay, Jim, Tom, Chris, Paul, Scott, Rizwan, Anita, Bill, Beau, Al, Doug ... thanks for your support and camaraderie over the years and all that we accomplished!

And to all my students to whom I have taught database management ... may this material take you to the next level!

Acknowledgments

Thanks to Dr. Chip Mason and Dr. Rick Upchurch for their support during this effort and for giving me the occasion to put this to print. I also want to thank those who supported me early on in this long-term project. Thanks to Alecia Gray for her editing work and for Sonya Weisser and Colin Brack for their professional opinions, much appreciated!

Special thanks go to; Dennis Chalupa, a former colleague, who contributed greatly to the chapter on queries, as well as Alison Gentry for major editing help.

Larry Ruddell
Houston, Texas
June, 2018

"I turned my heart to know and to search out and to seek wisdom and the scheme of things …"

Ecclesiastes 7:25a

Contents

Introduction

Congratulations! You are wise to take this journey into the fruitful world of database management. You will find this material valuable to you personally and professionally. Many working people have a passing knowledge of databases and can generate a few queries and reports. But very few working people actually understand databases and have a plan for how to use database tools to boost productivity and allow organizations to pull data for analysis and competitive advantage!

Several topics introduced in this book can be fleshed out in an entire class. For example, a class could be built on the history and theory of database design and the details of more advanced techniques (and database design tools) for building and managing databases and database administrator functions including security and user interface design. But it is better to have a holistic approach that covers all the pertinent topics that you need to know as a business leader. Knowledge gleaned from this book will more than get you started so that you can work right now in the database arena. You can then add more depth to your skills as required. But for many leaders, this material will be all that you need!

If you are reading this book, it tells me that you are serious about improving your career skills and marketability. Having expertise in the database arena will set you apart from other employees in the technical field and especially in any nontechnical field in which you choose to labor.

What is Database Management?

This book is about database management. But, let's start with **data**.

Data is a representation of business activity.

For example, you want to keep track of financial data like customer transactions (such things as what they bought, price of item and total spent). You want to keep track of operational data like inventory (such things as the name and number of a product you have in inventory, when you obtained it, how much you spent for it and how many you currently have of that product). This is called **Data management**.

Data management is your approach for keeping track of your business activities.

For example, you can use file folders, notebooks, your own daily planner or even sticky notes! However, it is much more efficient and effective to use an electronic way to store your data in a database, which we call **database management**.

Database management is using an electronic way to store and then use your business data.

A **Database Management System** (DBMS) is the specific software package that you use for data management; like Microsoft Access, FileMaker Pro, or SQL Server.

A Database Management System is the specific software package that you use for data management; like Microsoft Access.

And finally, a **database application** uses the special features in a DBMS, like Microsoft Access, to build an easy-to-use, menu-driven system that helps you, and especially users with less expertise, complete work faster and better.

A database application uses the special features in a DBMS like Microsoft Access to build an easy-to-use, menu-driven system.

Now that we have an understanding of basic terms, let's take a look at the goal and approach we will be using in the book.

Goal of This Book

The goal of this book is to equip you to lead the database function in your organization; either by doing it yourself or by overseeing others who do it.

Approach of This Book

The content of this book includes three basic elements:

1. A suggested plan (which we call our **Blueprint**) for finding and/or developing a database to capture, store, and retrieve data for running the business (operations) and/or for helping the organization make decisions (decision support and analytics).
2. Particular techniques in Microsoft Access to use in carrying out the Blueprint guidelines.
3. Organizational issues that a business leader needs to be aware of and manage.

You will learn the Blueprint as a guide to your database management efforts. If you understand the elements of the Blueprint, you should have a much better handle on how to manage your data. In each step of the Blueprint you will learn about the particular techniques (using examples from Microsoft Access) that you can use yourself to build (or oversee the building of) your own database. Also, perhaps even more importantly, you will gain more insight into understanding and using commercial databases. Throughout the book, you will also learn about the organizational issues that may affect your project. To set yourself apart from other people who play with database work, you will want to develop your expertise by working with a Blueprint, master techniques in carrying out the Blueprint, and then consider organizational issues while doing both.

You can then take these principles and use in many different situations and with other DBMSs. As we have stated previously, the focus is on business productivity; that's why we use computers. Your challenge is to constantly keep this goal of productivity in mind as you learn this material. Perhaps the most important point of the book is that **the database application needs to support your business and not vice versa**.

Effective learning must cover the forest (the "big picture") as well as the trees (details of "how to" do it). In this book we will go through the steps of how to understand and develop (if necessary) database applications but will do so from a business leadership point of view. This way, you will learn a skill (how to use the DBMS tools) but also learn the decision points involved with developing or buying and using a database application, which is important to you as a business leader.

Chapter 1 of the book gives a basic understanding of the "database world" which will introduce important terms and concepts to keep in mind as a business leader, including problems that typically come up. Chapter 2 covers the basic managerial decision to "make" or "buy" database application solutions and establishing specifications. It also reviews how to plan for working out your database solution. The rest of the chapters cover the Blueprint which you will need to know and understand regardless of whether or not you decide to "make" or "buy."

One final point; to grow in your expertise as a leader in managing data, you need to understand the appropriate terms as "tools of the trade." Each chapter includes a *Terms to Know* section which lists the terms introduced in that chapter. When the term is used in the chapter, the term appears in **bold** and the definition appears immediately below in *italics*. Also, it is recommended that you print out the **Glossary** in the back of the book and keep it with you. You can then refer to it as needed. It is not expected that you memorize all the terms but you should gain a familiarity with them so you can communicate effectively in the "database world."

Chapter 1
Understand the Database World

Chapter Overview

Maybe you are just beginning to design (or oversee the design of) your first database, or maybe you have experience in database concepts and applications but want to continue to build your skills. In either case, you need to understand the two basic kinds of organizations that you will work with; you need to understand what the roles are in the database world, particularly the three types of development roles; and as a business leader decide on who should take which of these roles in your organization. You will learn how people often approach database work and some of the pitfalls of those approaches. Finally, you will learn an effective blueprint for database application development that you will follow in the rest of the book.

Goals for Learning

- Understand the two basic kinds of organizations that you will work with.
- Learn about the three basic kinds of people in the database world.
- Learn about the four kinds of developer roles.
- Describe four problems that people often have when creating a database solution.
- Describe why a blueprint is important.
- State the parts of the database Blueprint.

Questions to Answer as You Read

1. What are the two basic kinds of organizations that you will work with? How are they similar? How are they different?
2. What are the three basic groups of people that you find in the database world?
3. What are the differences between power users and developers?
4. What are the four kinds of developer roles that you can take? Which roup of developers do you best fit into and why?
5. Give three examples of the transaction processing database function.
6. Give two examples of the management information database function.
7. Give one example of the decision support database function.
8. What are four problems that people often have when creating a database solution? How do you think you can avoid these problems?
9. What is the Systems Development Cycle approach to database development? What are some advantages and some disadvantages to this approach?
10. What is the Prototype approach to database development? What are some advantages and some disadvantages to this approach?
11. Why is a blueprint important?
12. What are the parts of our database Blueprint?

Terms to Know

Take time to review these terms in the Glossary section at the back of the book:

Analytics
Blueprint
Business processes
Business rules
CASE
Database platform
Decision Support system

Developers
Enterprise Resource Planning (ERP) System
Error checking
Information Systems (IS) group
Management Information system
Power Users
Program
Prototype
Rollback
Successful applications
Transaction Processing system
Users
View
Workgroup

Two Kinds of Organizations

To understand where you fit into the database world, you must first understand a little about the "geography" of that world. We will look at large companies and small companies. In the next section, we will examine the different roles that you can play in these two different arenas.

Large Companies

Large companies often rely on an **Enterprise Resource Planning (ERP)** system to meet their informational requirements.

> *Enterprise Resource Planning (ERP) systems are database applications used by large companies to manage all of their daily activities.*

ERPs are large and costly; and often times they force a set of processes on a company (which may or may not actually help business operations). They also require a large amount of control and security. Organizations put procedures in place to make sure that the ERP works properly. Because of the importance of the ERP system, the **Information Systems (IS) group**, focuses (rightly) on this application.

> *The Information Systems (IS) group OR Information Technology (IT) group is the organizational group that supports technology hardware and software and infrastructure, including database administration.*

The policies of the IS group can then be driven by this approach; as they do not want people to have access to certain parts of the data or have the capability of building their own database solutions. They tell people to "let the professional do it." Talented developers (the experts) work in the IS group but may not have time (or be willing to take time) to meet user requests for other types of data.

People react in two different ways to this barrier. First, people wait for the IS group to respond to their request. This delay often thwarts productivity by not allowing people to obtain critical information at the right time. Secondly, others grow frustrated and build their own databases. However, they have no time to fully learn the tools. They need coaching but there is no plan by the experts to provide the needed coaching. Also, there is no communication with others who are in the same predicament, so several different groups may attempt very different solutions to similar work problems. The former results in wasted time while the latter results in wasted time and duplicated effort.

Large organizations need trained database developers who can work on large, formal applications. But, they also need database developers peppered throughout the organization who can create **workgroup** database solutions for departments.

> *A workgroup is a group of approximately two to thirty people who work in a specific task area in an organization.*

Will you meet the need?

Small Companies

Small companies also have database problems. The leaders of small companies often lack expertise in database work. They also lack the resources to hire a full-time database person, so, they fulfill their database needs by buying commercial programs to carry out their various business functions such as accounting, sales, and service. This is useful, but limited, because it often cannot provide the variety of reports they may require. They may be willing to pay for database consulting but normally on a limited scale; wanting the "most bang for the buck."

If small business owners do any custom database work, it is often redundant and hard to manage. They are also under severe time constraints so don't have time to "do it right." Small business owners often need coaching so that they can provide guidelines for database consultants and/or manage their data effectively. Also, ideally, another staff person can be equipped to help.

One effective solution for small organizations is to find an experienced database consultant who can work with canned commercial applications and can develop additional parts to meet information requirements.

Your Place in the Database World

As you enter the database development world, it can prove overwhelming or exhilarating. For those who may feel overwhelmed at delving into this arena, take heart. By working through the material in this book, you will learn everything you need to know to build basic database applications. For those of you who are strong technically, this book will present you with a different challenge. It will challenge you to continually focus your database work on productivity instead of merely exploring "neat features" of a particular product (in our case Microsoft Access). Believe me, you will learn about some awesome features of Access. Your challenge is to understand and determine which features will prove to be useful on a particular work requirement. This is a skill that supersedes mere technical knowledge of a product. You must pursue productivity and ignore "rabbit trails" that often lead developers to pursue interesting but irrelevant features of a product.

This book will help you understand which Access features and techniques will move you towards productivity, which is fundamental to leadership.

Three Basic Groups

You can be a part of this database revolution that both large and small companies require. What part will you play? In order to determine your place in the revolution, you must understand the three basic groups of people in the database world: users, power users and developers.

Users

Database **users** play an important role in the database world.

Users are people who use databases that other people create.

Users perform a very important role in entering and editing data, running processes, printing reports and using the information generated from the database. It is essential to train users on the basics of using a particular database program. For example, users who work with Microsoft Access applications should:

- Learn how to use the Access **Find** feature.
- Understand how to use a **Filter**.
- Know how to tell the difference between Form **view** and Datasheet view.

In Microsoft Access, this refers to different ways of looking at data or design (i.e. switching between Design View and Datasheet View). It can also refer to a particular subset of data that you are looking at.

Keep in mind that users are only expected to use and understand the features that someone teaches them.

Power Users

Power users can play an important role in organizations.

Power users know how to work from the Access Database Window to find answers to questions and report the results.

Power users know how to examine data in table design, and how to locate and use data from large systems and other data sources. Power user skills are very helpful because they can create custom queries to answer ad hoc questions that arise and create custom reports to format the answers. They know how to work efficiently in Access query design and report design.

Developers

Developers play a very important role in the database world.

Developers create database applications that users can work with.

They understand how to work effectively in Access form design and can automate Access actions with buttons and menus. This book will help you become an effective Access power user and developer.

Four Kinds of Developers

Which of the three database groups do you fall into? If you are reading this book, it is obvious that you want to work as a developer. Now that you are ready to move into this elite company, let's examine the four types of developers:

1. Experts who write the books on the application software.
2. Large System professional developers who work on ERP systems.
3. Small System professional developers who work on workgroup solutions for large companies and applications for small companies.

4. Content experts who build applications for personal use and provide workgroup solutions for large companies or specialized applications for small companies according to their content expertise.

Experts

Experts are tremendous resources for learning the idiosyncrasies of a certain product, for obtaining techniques for certain development situations, and for thinking through the future possibilities of a product. Often these experts helped build the database product or were part of the evaluation team who decided to make or buy the product in the first place.

Large System Professional Developers

Large system professional developers work on supporting and/or replacing ERP systems. They work exclusively on large development projects with a team of other people. The applications they build need to work flawlessly and seamlessly. This means that these large system professionals use a database design tool to generate and maintain the database structure, put in place security, add thorough error checking, complete coding for transaction processing, maintain version control documentation, appoint a database administrator to oversee security and database maintenance, complete help and documentation (normally done by a separate individual on the team), and support the system after it is completed. Normally, workers in this arena have a computer science background. All development work is coded. Some of the readers of this book will fall into this category.

Small System Professional Developers

The third group of developers work as small system professional developers, producing workgroup solutions for large companies and applications for small companies. Some people in this group also include content experts who have special expertise in database development. They may work alone or with one or two other developers. They often use data that is already in place to create decision support types of reports. They also may develop a database to capture additional data that is not maintained by the ERP system or by business software to help track distinct business data.

This additional database can then be used as a management information system in conjunction with the other data. Applications at this level do not have to include all of the features of the databases developed by the large system professionals because they are servicing a smaller group of users with smaller needs. Changes can be implemented readily because the developer works closely with the workers. The developer can also train the users on how to use the application, so that the application does not have to be as versatile. A minimum level of security (if any) may be required. Developers may use a combination of macros (discussed later) and coding to complete their project. Many of the readers of the book will fall into this category.

Content Experts

The fourth group of developers are content experts who build applications for personal use and provide workgroup solutions for large companies or specialized applications for small companies according to their content expertise. This group is similar to the previous group, but they do not have to pay as much attention to detail in their development. They work primarily with macros or simple code to create their automated solution. Very little, if any, **error checking** is present and no concern is given to security.

> *Writing code to check potential errors that might occur and provide a user-friendly way to work out the problem. Error checking can also be called error trapping.*

A number of readers of this book will fall into this category.

What Will You Develop?

Now that you know what kind of developer you will be (or oversee!), it is important to understand what kinds of database applications you will develop. The first personal computer (PC) DBMS I ever used was called *dBase II*. When you opened up dBase II, you saw a period. That's it, a period.

You might say that you saw a period, *period*. To do anything, you had to type in commands such as:

- Use <database name>
- Append
- Quit

The beauty of dBase II was that you could write **programs** to create menus, add data, edit data, carry out calculations, search for information, and generate reports.

> *A computer program is a set of individual instructions that tell the computer what to do.*

You had much flexibility. I soon learned techniques for making all of these things happen and much more. As I continued to work with other databases including FoxPro, Paradox, Sybase, Access and SQL Server, for example; I found that the techniques were very similar. I also found that I could use a similar approach when using any database product to create **successful applications**.

> *A successful application, is one that is useful to the organization, done in a timely way, and that people actually use.*

Before we look at our **Blueprint**, let's review the different functions of database systems that you will develop. This will help you decide what techniques to use in building your database application.

> *A blueprint is an overall plan of design.*

There are three basic functions of databases that you will create. Your application may include one or all of these functions. But it is important to discriminate between them. The three functions are: **Transaction Processing, Management Information** and **Decision Support**.

Transaction Processing Systems are database applications that store, retrieve, and process data required for basic business activities.

Management Information Systems work with Transaction Processing database applications to help manage and carry out business data activities for you.

Decision Support Systems use your DBMS to pull data from many different places to help you make decisions.

Let's examine each one and see what they do.

Transaction Processing

Transaction Processing is the formal name for what database systems normally do. This includes adding information, editing information, finding information, calculating information, summarizing information, and reporting basic information. Some examples of transaction processing functions include:

- Managing a phone list.
- Keeping track of legal cases.
- Tracking reservations for a training class.
- Entering sales.

In a phone list you add names, find people so that you can call them, make changes, send out mailings to certain groups of people on the list, and print out a phone directory. The transaction processing function is identified by the fact that you are storing and retrieving the same information in different views.

Components of the transaction processing function include:

- Using Forms to add, edit, delete and find information.
- Creating Queries to run calculations and to summarize data.
- Creating Reports consisting of lists of information.
- Creating Reports consisting of grand totals and subtotals.

Your users will normally carry out the transaction processing function more often than any other. However, in many cases bar codes, QR codes, or even customer apps are used to enter transactions. Most databases that you develop will include this functionality, which is probably the easiest, but most tedious, to build. It is easy in that many of the database application features that you need to create in order to add, edit, delete, or find information are easy to create. It is tedious because it takes time to set up forms, create queries, and lay out reports. Because the transaction processing function is so common, you can often reuse forms and code that you create. Later in the book, you will learn some of these basic techniques needed to add transaction processing functionality to your database application.

Keep in mind that your transaction processing development techniques are more difficult due to three factors. These three factors are best identified by asking three basic questions:

1. How many people will access the data at the same time?
2. Where are the people located? Are they all in the same office or scattered throughout several countries?
3. How many people will make changes to the data at the same time?

If many people will access the data at the same time or the people are scattered throughout several locations or many people will make changes to the data at the same time, then you need to use a different set of database development techniques. Also, you need to change your **platform**.

> *The database platform is the Operating System, the computer and network, the database software on which the data is kept and stored.*

Management Information

Management Information describes the process of using your database system to do work for you. For example, you can set up your database to maintain your inventory and tell you when to reorder materials when they dwindle. In the old days, you would count this inventory manually each day or week and have to remind yourself when to take action and order more of a certain material. Adding management information capabilities means that the database will keep track of the inventory for you. For example, your database will automatically change the inventory count after you make a sale. You can set up a reorder level for your materials, which the database will check after you subtract the order amount. Then your database system will tell you which materials to reorder or even place an order directly with a designated vendor if your value chain is tightly integrated.

There is another focus on MIS. This is where pertinent data is gathered via queries and reports and delivered to managers so that they can make decisions. There can be overlap between database transaction activity and the MIS functions. The main thing is that MIS helps managers manage!

Normally management information capabilities are added to a transaction processing system. Adding management information capabilities can prove more complex than transaction processing functions in that you have to clarify **business rules** so that your database responds according to these rules.

> *Business rules are written (or understood) guidelines of what happens in a company. For example, a business rule for invoice payment might read: "We pay all invoices that are two weeks old or older on the last Friday of the month."*

These rules will differ from situation to situation. For example, in a parking garage management application (a project I worked on), you need to set up rules for how people are charged for part of a month. The system then decides the amount to charge a customer when you enter a date for the parking sign up. The user does not have to sit down and calculate the amount for each situation; the database application does it automatically.

Sometimes management information and transaction processing functions intersect; as in keeping an inventory, for example. Suppose you make a sale and start to print the packing slip. You set up the inventory update to take place after the packing slip prints. The printer jams and your application freezes, creating a problem. You made a sale, but the database did not subtract the items from inventory. Adding **rollback** to your application, an advanced transaction processing technique, will make sure that your database will not record a sale if the items are not deducted from inventory.

> *Rollback happens when changing several pieces of data; if all the changes do not take place as planned, all of the changes are undone and reset to their original values, thus protecting the integrity of the data.*

Decision Support

Decision Support describes the process of pulling data from many different places to help you make big decisions. Management information makes immediate decisions for you, based on rules you build in. With decision support, you normally draw from different data sources in your organization and even outside your organization. You might want to answer a question such as: when is the best time for us to build a new building to handle our growth? Or, is it better to rent temporary space? Graphs and charts are useful in this mode. Often it is helpful to move data into a spreadsheet to present different *What if?* scenarios. For example, when deciding on space, you might want to look at the impact on profitability over the next five years between buying a new building (with added production capabilities) versus renting space.

Queries form the foundation of the decision support database function. The database development for a decision support system is not complex (since you are using data you already have) but the conceptual analysis is. Your challenge is to locate the proper data, to pull it into one place, and to set up queries that properly answer your questions.

Data **analytics** is another decision support system but on a much larger scale and using additional types of data (like clicks on a website).

> *Using internal and external data in traditional and non-traditional formats to develop and test hypotheses for solving business problems.*

However, the fundamental data design and query principles that we will discuss later in the book are still useful in pulling together "big data" for analysis.

Five Classic Problems Database Developers Face

Before we look at solid approaches to database design, it is helpful (and somewhat humorous) to look at five classic problems that database developers face in defining and carrying out their work. By identifying these problems, I trust that you will gain wisdom so that you will avoid them in the future.

To Tell the Truth

In this ancient TV variety show, three people emerged from behind a curtain claiming to be the same person. They then answered questions about what this person did. The panel asked questions of the three people to determine the real person from the two impostors. Then came the climax. The host asked the question: *will the real person please stand up?* The moment of truth came when the real person slowly rose up from their seat. Often the panel was completely misled by the comments of the impostors.

In database development, you often begin building a database for a particular person. Half way through your project you slowly realize that the person you ostensibly are working for is not the real person who actually approves the work. You continually try to find out who is the real person for whom you are doing the work. You try to meet the requirements of various people, none of whom is the person who has the authority to give the final approval for the work. This approach is frustrating for everyone involved; the developer, the users, and the real person who gives final approval.

Name It and Claim It

The project starts out innocently enough. The developer does the required work. But invariably when you present the work, it is not quite enough. Users request changes that they did not mention previously. The requested changes can be cosmetic; how the application looks. Or they can be more involved. Many times, they want additional functionality that you did not discuss previously.

Many people provide input as to what the application should do, but there is not one person who takes responsibility for stopping the onslaught.

This is different from *To Tell the Truth* because more users are involved and they like your work. The problem is that they continually want more than was expected.

Runaway

The developer obtains general directions from his customer and takes off. The goal in development quickly becomes "how do I use an interesting programming technique for this?" In focusing on development techniques, the developer loses sight of the main goal: to meet business requirements. He creates this situation by not listening carefully to the users and by not having regular checkpoints where the users approve the work. The difference in this problem is that the developer creates the problems versus the user.

Walk the Plank (Or Three Blind Mice)

People who have worked with a database development tool for a few hours see themselves as experts and "build a database." They then invite you to "walk" in and modify (or fix) it. You "walk the plank" with this approach because it is difficult to know what is really going on with the database and when it is not going to work. The added danger is that the developer might actually think that it does work.

The Never-Ending Story

Application development continues on because it is never quite right. Because the application is still "in process," the organization gains no productivity from the time that has been spent. Users (and sometimes developers) hope that the application will do "one more thing." As the application grows more complex, there is more chance that things can go wrong. When the application is finally installed, users do not want to take the time to learn it. Little effort is made to teach them and show them the benefits of the new database, so no one uses it. The entire process then returns to the state mentioned in the first sentence of this paragraph.

Two Approaches to Database Development

There are better ways! Let's examine two basic approaches to database development that emerge from some of the writing on database development:

1. Systems Development Cycle.
2. Prototype Approach.

Systems Development Cycle

The systems development cycle is a formal and detailed process of defining user requirements and carrying out development. This approach is formal in that it is normally highly structured, it takes a long time to implement and it involves many people. Organizations use this approach for developing large systems that normally take longer than six months to complete. The data captured and manipulated by the system is usually predictable and repetitive. For example, you might use this approach to develop a new accounting system for an energy company, to create a parking and leasing billing system for a property management firm, or to set up an on-line ticketing service for an airline.

The systems development cycle is laid out in great detail because of the number of steps you have to complete to carry out the process. You spend a great deal of time developing the requirements. For example, you might include the following steps in your approach (Senn, 1987):

- Formulation of Master Plan
  - o Systems need
  - o Clarification of purpose
  - o Feasibility assessment
    - Assessment of technical feasibility
    - Assessment of economic feasibility
    - Assessment of operational feasibility
- Requirements analysis
  - o Determination of user information needs
  - o Description of user needs
  - o Setting detailed system requirements

- Logical systems design
  - o Specification of procedures
  - o Specification of input/output
  - o Specification of files and databases
- Physical systems development
  - o Development of files and databases
- Testing
  - o Procedure testing
  - o File and space testing
- Implementation and evaluation
- Training conversion
- Maintenance
- Assessment of new system.

The particular techniques used in the process can vary depending on the goal of the application and the particular tools used. Note that the above example includes a stage for feasibility study in the *Formulation of Master Plan* phase. Because this technique is normally used on very large systems that affect most of the people in a multi-departmental organization, much work may be needed to determine if the project should be undertaken. Many people are involved in the decision-making process, so there can be a problem with organizational and communication issues.

Most system design approaches use some form of Computer Aided System Engineering (**CASE**) technology for carrying out their design.

> *CASE (Computer Aided Software Engineering) uses software to model business activities and then translates into database application objects, primarily tables.*

It is a piece of software that guides you through the process of graphically laying out **business processes** (the actual work).

> *Business processes are the activities which occur on a regular basis in an organization to carry out its operations.*

Then it designs a database structure that will capture those requirements. In some cases, a CASE tool can also build and maintain the database. There are several CASE software applications on the market: EasyCASE, ERWin, InfoModeler and even Microsoft Visio. ProVision is particularly useful in capturing and modeling business processes. These tools differ but all of them are designed to help you capture what is important in an organization and then lay out the data and user interface needed to translate the work into a database that reflects the work situation.

Unfortunately, because of their complexity, it is time consuming to learn how to use CASE tools and apply them. In fact, you almost have to focus on one particular tool and master that tool. This limits your flexibility in working with other types of systems design approaches. The other problem is that using the tool can be an end in itself. It takes time to follow each step of the systems design process and to properly document it. Developers can grow wooden and lose flexibility in adapting to new organizational requirements. This approach is most useful for large, organization-wide applications that are relatively predictable.

Prototype Approach

The **prototype** approach to database development is different.

A prototype is a working example presented to the client for feedback.

This approach involves talking to your users and then building a working example of what they want. The users then use the application, communicate about any desired changes, and then you modify the database based on the requested changes and any problems that you encounter. You repeat these steps until you complete your application. As you change the working example, it slowly but surely grows into the final product. Instead of using CASE tools to analyze and plan your work, you simply start creating your application.

You will find several advantages to using the prototype approach:

- Flexible: Most applications change because work changes. The prototype approach keeps you from spending a great deal of time designing a system that will change. You can adapt quickly to your changing database requirements by directly modifying the application.

- Welcomes feedback: The prototype approach to database application development welcomes feedback. The responses you obtain from users provide the foundation to this development approach. The feedback determines the changes you make to the database. This is ongoing.

- Focuses on the task and not the process: The systems design approach can prove tedious. You follow structured steps to complete your design and carry out your development. Sometimes you can focus too much on the design process and lose sight of the end result: building an application. The prototype approach focuses on results. You have little danger of growing bogged down with maintaining your design.

The prototype approach will be a useful addition to your professional arsenal. However, you need to be aware of some limitations of this technique.

- Can result in much reworking: Because you do not spend as much time in planning, you can run into unpredictable results. For example, you can create your database application and then realize that you left out a crucial field in your table design. Or, you realize that you need to move several fields in a table to a new table. You will need much time to fix this problem because you have already created queries, forms, reports, and coding without using these fields properly.

- You may not take into account all of the requirements: You may begin your work based on conversations with one group of users. After finishing the prototype, you may find that other people have a different set of requirements that may conflict with the original group.

- Can encourage a sloppy approach to planning: Because the prototype approach is very flexible, you may not take the time needed to talk to users about their needs. Also, because you know that you will change the design, you may not take care to lay out your different objects properly. This can cause problems in following the design and maintaining the application.

The prototype approach can prove useful when you are building relatively small applications with a few users who are knowledgeable. However, the prototype approach can be like building the frame of a new building before pouring the concrete for the ground floor. The frame has nothing to attach to. The building will probably totter significantly and may even fall altogether from a brisk wind. The elements can do damage to the frame without a floor. You may be able to pour the concrete later, but it will prove difficult. If you start building an application without carefully defining what you want to accomplish at the start, you can run into problems later.

The Blueprint

The approach you use to develop and/or oversee your database applications will vary depending on what you want to accomplish. However, as a business leader overseeing database management, you need some straightforward approach that will guide you to a successful completion of your project. This Blueprint takes the basics of the systems design and prototype approaches in order to provide you with a framework applicable to any situation where you are responsible for finding or developing, installing and supporting a database application.

Our approach is detailed below. The rest of the book will involve developing each one of these parts.

- Part 1 – Plan your work
- Part 2 - Set up tables to store your data
- Part 3 - Create queries and reports
- Part 4 - Set up forms to capture data
- Part 5 - Set up forms to run the application
- Part 6 - Add code to tie the application together
- Part 7 - Implement

The rest of the chapters of the book cover each of these parts in detail.

Be reminded that the Blueprint is pertinent for even commercial systems. For example, you still need to complete Step 1 and if the commercial database application doesn't do what your business needs, you need to find another way to meet the requirement (i.e. by using the hybrid approach of creating a database application to meet the requirement that draws from data from the commercial database application).

Chapter Review

Maybe you are just beginning to design your first database, or maybe you have experience in database concepts and applications but want to continue to build your skills. In either case, you need to understand the two basic kinds of organizations that you will work with; you need to understand what the roles are in the database world, particularly the three types of development roles; you need to decide which of these roles you want to fill in the database world, and what you want to accomplish in the role that you choose. You then need to avoid the common pitfalls of database development and find a dependable approach for working in the database world.

Chapter 2
Plan Your Work

Chapter Overview

Chapter 2 explains how to plan your work by laying out your specifications. Part of planning involves the decision to make or buy your database application. This decision will impact how you plan; but either way, you must be clear on the work your organization does.

You will learn an efficient method for defining database requirements. We will illustrate this method by giving specific examples. You will learn to avoid time wasters and to embrace the importance of scope definition. You will learn guidelines for estimating the time it will take you to create a database application.

This chapter also explains how to use database standards and why they are important. The chapter will also show you how to make your communication more efficient by knowing what parts of your database work to standardize and when.

Goals for Learning

- Clarify the difference between *making* versus *buying* a database application.
- Understand the importance of laying out accurate and relevant database development specifications.
- Understand what a proposal does for you.
- Learn how to establish database solution specifications by creating a proposal.

Plan Your Work

- Learn how to define the scope of your work.
- Learn how to make time estimations.
- Create a proposal.
- Understand the purpose and function of database standards.
- Learn an approach to standards with Access.

Questions to Answer as You Read

1. What are specifications?
2. Why is it important to lay out accurate and relevant database development specifications?
3. What are two perspectives for laying out specifications and how might they complement each other?
4. What are the three attitude qualities that distinguish you as a professional?
5. What are the five steps that make up this Planning phase of the Blueprint?
6. What are the four groups of people that you need to interact with in setting up your team? How do you include each group in the planning process?
7. What can you do to discover what work needs to be done?
8. What does a proposal do for you?
9. What do you include in a proposal?
10. What is scope of work? Why is this important?
11. Give three techniques for estimating time for database development. Which one do you recommend and why?
12. What is the purpose of adopting database standards?
13. What are three areas where you should follow naming conventions?

Terms to Know

Take time to review these terms in the Glossary section at the back of the book:

Assumptions
Change order
Client

Contingency

Control

Database Development standards

DBA (Database Administrator)

Decision makers

Documentation

Duration

Entity

Fixed price bid

Lookup table

Main database object

Milestone

Object

Object description

PERT

Phase

Project management

Proposal

Roll out

Scope

Specifications

Switchboard

System tables

Task

Technical Support personnel

Variables

Work

Make versus Buy?

As a business leader, you are faced with information technology (IT) decisions. You have to decide on, for example; operating system, business software for your organization, hardware, internet services and, the focus of this book, a DBMS. When making value chain decisions about your business, the basic question to ask is whether you want to handle some or all of the steps in the value chain or do you want to pay someone else to handle that step. A basic example would be a coffee company. Do you want to actually grow your own beans and take care of the shipping and processing of those beans; or do you want to pay someone else to do that based on your quality standards? The trade-offs are between control and risk and also cost. In other words, if you grow your own coffee beans, you have control over the whole growing process (for quality purposes), but you also assume the risk involved (i.e. if there is bad weather, disease or even governmental constraints over control of the land); as well as financial considerations (i.e. if you grow your own beans, you need to invest in farm equipment, find land to purchase, hire workers and build units for cleaning and preparing the beans for shipment … to name a few).

The same concept applies to your database application choice. You have to decide on whether or not you want to develop your own database application or buy a product that someone else has developed. In this case, the trade-offs are the same; related to cost and risk and control. Let's look at the trade-offs in more detail and why you might want to make or buy your next database application for your organization.

Buy Decision

First of all, let's examine why you might want to buy your database application. As mentioned above, you reduce risk that comes from developing your own since the vendor is taking that risk. They will make sure that the application works and is updated and normally will provide support if you have any issues or problems. They might also provide training. Normally a commercial database application will have most of the features that you need to run your business, or at least parts of it.

Also, leaders in the organization may not want to "rock the boat," so they want to buy something "established" versus trying something new; which, again, may be more a perception of risk versus a reality; but it still holds true. Users expect their technology to work perfectly, so are impatient with new and different systems (no matter how useful), especially if there are any problems during roll out. Often times a commercial package is already Web deployed which is a good thing. Also, security (and/or the ability to set security) is normally built in which is a big help. Finally, the commercial company provides trained technical personnel to support the application, which manages the personnel risk (risk of having a key person leave your company).

Make Decision

There are some reasons for making your own database application. If the requirements are fairly simple and the number of users is small and localized, then it may well be more cost effective to create your own database.

Commercial packages have disadvantages as well. Commercial vendors can build hooks (switching costs) into their services, which makes it difficult and expensive to get rid of them. You may even have difficulty obtaining your data when severing relationships with a commercial vendor, so it is important to work out all of these possibilities before purchasing. Also, sometimes commercial vendors sell their database applications in separate systems or parts (where you pay extra for functionality you need), which adds to the cost.

Another issue is the functionality of a commercial product. The commercial product may not give you all the functionality you need to run your organization and may give you many functions that you don't need. A custom application gives you exactly what you need, nothing more and nothing less; and you can add to it should requirements change.

Hybrid Approach

Another approach to selecting a database application is a hybrid approach, which has a strong upside. The hybrid approach involves selecting a commercial product that provides most of the functionality you need, and then supplementing the commercial database application with additional parts (or systems) that are made; using the commercial data as the foundation. This approach allows you to fill in the data gaps while reaping the benefits from having a commercial application.

The priority in purchasing a commercial database application should be given to the marketing function (customer management and sales) as most data management revolves around customer relationship development and sales. There also has to be a way to interact with your accounting system, i.e.

for posting sales. In examining potential products, make sure to ask about the data structure and format and where the data is stored. At minimum, you should be able to download your data from the vendor whenever you need it. It is better if you can directly attach (or *link*) to the data (will be discussed later in the book) but may not be possible.

For example, *ergo, Inc.* (name has been changed) is an ergonomics company (small business) that I worked with. They have unique data needs that focus on their operations. They have specific criteria they use to evaluate customers and their ergonomic needs. This required a database application that *ergo* could use at the customer site to enter customer responses to a diagnostic questionnaire and then generate a report summarizing the results and providing recommendations based on those results. Since the company runs on a Mac platform, FileMaker Pro (can run on Mac or Windows platform) was selected as the DBMS. A custom database application was then built and tested with some benefit, however there were functionality issues. After consideration, the owner was able to locate an IT company that was interested in developing and commercializing the application that ergo needed. They have moved ahead and developed a successful solution for both (IT company providing solutions for ergo and ergo marketing the application to clients).

The Most Important Piece of Information

When considering whether to make or buy your database application, you need to keep the most important piece of information in mind and that is answering the question: how, exactly, does your business work and how do you want it to work? As a business leader, you will have major problems with data management if you do not clarify exactly how your business should operate. Remember, the data simply represents what is important to your actual business. The database should serve your business purposes and not vice versa. Organizations will buy a database application to get "organized" and then (after much cost and effort) have difficulty deploying the application because they don't know how their business works which only leads to confusion and inefficiency.

Where to Go from Here

In summary, whether you make or buy your database application; you definitely need to know your business. Once you know your business, you are then ready to lay out requirements for your database application. In the pages that follow, we will discuss a blueprint for how to understand databases and how to use them to obtain information. Whether you make or buy your database application, to be an effective business leader, you need to know how it works. These details will help you learn to develop your own database applications and/or use other data that might come from a commercial application so you can run your business. Remember, the data simply reflects your actual business. So, start by making sure a commercial application actually captures the data you need. If not (or there are gaps), consider developing your own database application. Remember, the database application is there to serve your business and not vice versa.

One more thing before we jump in: the rest of the book focuses on steps (Blueprint for Success) for developing a database application. We do this for two reasons. One; you may well want to have that skill set so you can develop database applications for your organization or as a consultant, and two; if you understand how to develop database applications, you will learn the tools for assessing and using a commercial database application. Finally, you will learn features of Microsoft Access which you can use to develop applications and/or as a tool for pulling together data from a commercial and/or other organizational source (like Excel).

What Are Specifications?

You receive a phone call. Jill needs you to build a "database" to track training activities. Where do you begin? How do you peer into Jill's head to find out what she means by "database"? How will you make sure that you give her what she needs? We will address all of these questions and many more during this first part of our Blueprint: *Plan Your Work*, which starts with identifying **specifications**.

A specification is a visual and/or written statement that describes what work your database will do for the people in your organization and the database features you will build to accomplish this work objective.

There are two parts to this definition. First of all, you need to define exactly what work the organization is doing and how. You need to define this work from the point of view of the people in the organization; not just your own. In other words, it has to be REAL. After you write down what work they want to accomplish, they should be able to look at what you write and say, "Yes, this is what we want to accomplish in our work."

Secondly, you then need to translate this explanation of the organizational work into database development terms. For example, the people might tell you that they need to schedule classes accurately and efficiently. This is the first aspect of the specification. You then move to the second aspect of the specification which means you translate this desire to schedule classes into database terms: you need a class table and a schedule table in your database design. Depending on what they mean by "schedule classes," you also may need an instructor table, a classroom table, and a student table.

The word *specification* comes from the word *specific* which means *exact* or *precise.* Change takes place in the particulars of life, not in broad generalities. We live in a world where people do not like to be pinned down to specific commitments. We like to keep our options open. Some of this ethos is good. Businesses grow and change. We need to be able to adapt to some of those particular changes in our business or organization. However, a business or organization will eventually fail if it has no sense of purpose; if it is not able to clearly state what it wants to do and how it is different from other companies in the market. Your specifications need to reflect those aspects of the work that capture this essential purpose of the organization. They need to be very clear.

Remember the two perspectives of your specifications:

1. First perspective: Work accomplishment, also called the *logical* design, describes what work your database will do for your organization.
2. Second perspective: Database development, also called the *physical* design, focuses on the database features you will build to accomplish the work objective.

For example, if you are building a database application (also sometimes just called *database* as a short-cut) to keep track of proposals for an engineering firm, one specification might read: "Generate and track all proposals produced for customers." Make this happen by developing a customer table and form to keep track of customers; developing a proposal table and form to keep track of proposals; making a customer pick list item on the proposal form so that each proposal is tied to the proper customer; and creating a form with a subform to look at all outstanding proposals per customer. Notice the two aspects of the above example:

1. Work accomplishment: Gives the work requirement, i.e. *Generate and track all proposals produced for customers.*
2. Database development: Gives the details of exactly how you plan to build your database to accomplish this work requirement.

You might say that you are acting as an *interpreter* when you lay out specifications. A good interpreter first of all understands what the speaker says. They then speak this information in a different language so that the listener can understand. In developing your specifications, you must understand exactly what work your client wants to accomplish. Your job is then to interpret the work need into specific database tables, user interface (forms), actions (queries and code), and outputs (reports) so you have a guide for building the database that actually fulfills the work requirement.

Many people often use a certain technique to diagram the work accomplishment part of the specifications; called **Entity-Relationship diagramming**.

> *An Entity-Relationship diagram shows the items in the organization, how they relate to one another, and perhaps how this activity in the organization translates into data design.*

Entity is a fancy way of saying "people or things in your organization."

> *An entity is simply some aspect of the organization that is necessary to accomplish work.*

In our scheduling example; the class is an entity and the scheduling of the class is an action involving the entity.

This role of interpretation, historically, is performed by a special person called a *system engineer, systems analyst,* or a variety of other names. If you are working on a large project, a team of people will probably work solely on this aspect of the Blueprint – laying out specifications. However, as a database developer you need to understand and possess this skill. Building specifications is an art. This capability will set you apart from other leaders. If you know how to create databases and further also know how to listen, understand, and build specifications; you will prove very valuable to any organization with which you choose to work.

Why Is It Important to Lay Out Accurate and Relevant Specifications?

Normally you will have several specifications per database development project. Specifications serve as guidelines for your database development effort. They are important for several reasons:

- They help you understand why you are doing this work.
- They give detailed instructions on what you will do.
- They provide guidelines on how you will do the database development.
- They clarify who participates in the project.
- They pinpoint when the work is actually completed.
- They make sure you focus on the company work goals.

More importantly, they serve as a covenant (a sober commitment with benefits and accountability) between the developers and the organization specifying exactly what will be done and what the database will do.

Specifications manage expectations. Many projects fail because of false expectations from the developer or the **client** or the user (described previously).

> *The client is the person or persons who ask you do the work and sign off on the work.*

It is like trying to reach a particular destination by car. You could take off on your trip and meander your way down the road, taking turns that you feel will lead you in the right direction. You might arrive at your destination. But, at best you will take detours, side roads that slow you down, and possibly you will even go in the wrong direction at points before arriving. At worst, you will not even reach your destination. If you simply take a moment to look at a road map, you can go directly to the proper destination. You know generally how long the trip will take because you can see the distance and type of road on the map.

This first step is a critical one in our Blueprint for development. All the other parts of the Blueprint focus on the specifications. This is the only step in the Blueprint where you focus primarily on the business and what work you want to accomplish for the business or organization. It is important that you get this right. All the other steps of the Blueprint flow from this definition. If this is wrong, you may build a beautiful database application, but it will prove relatively useless.

It's like the time I was working a summer job during college at a service shop in Charlotte, North Carolina. I was told to take a truck and pick up a motor at another location; or so I thought. So, I filled up the truck with gasoline and took off down the highway. It was a beautiful day. The sun was shining. The birds were singing. The cool breeze bathed my face. I was making great time. I knew I would take care of this important assignment in no time. Forty minutes into the trip, I was blithely bouncing along when my buddy from work pulled alongside me in a different truck and motioned for me to stop. I stopped. He calmly said, "you forgot something," and pointed to the motor in the back of his truck. Reality set in like a cold shower early in the morning. I was supposed to deliver the motor, not pick it up. Later that day, after I cowered back to the shop, I received a serious lesson in the use of descriptive language! Where are you driving with your database development? Did you remember the client work requirements? Never forget the motor!

In summary, the specifications that you set up act as your road map to guide you to your database development destination. And remember your development destination; accomplishing work for the organization.

Your Attitude in Defining Specifications

Now that you understand what specifications are and why they are important, let's discuss how to garner database development specifications. There are several different general guidelines that you need to be aware of and specific techniques that you can use to obtain specifications. But before plunging into your action steps, you need to take a step back and look at your attitude as you begin the process of laying out specifications. Your attitude plays an important role in this process.

Visualize yourself as a famous detective. You listen. You dig for clues. You gather information to solve the case. You ward off threats to you and the case that you are working on. You communicate. You persist. You carry out interviews. You sit and think about the information you receive to see how it all fits together. You finally figure out who committed the crime, how they carried it out, and how to arrest the criminal. You are the database detective. You will ask the right questions. You will take nothing for granted. You will interview all of the right people. You will get to the bottom of the real business need of the organization you are serving and you will define that need clearly. You will have the right balance between humility and confidence. You will come as a servant. But you will insist on agreement at the proper time for the good of your client and your own good.

This tongue-in-cheek description about attitude underlines the importance of your personal relationship skills in developing database specifications. Completing database work requires you to interact with a wide range of people. You must carry yourself like a professional. What does it mean to work professionally? Keep in mind the following three attitude qualities that distinguish you as a professional:

1. Make sure that you communicate with the right people: If some action that you take will affect someone else, you let them know about it.
2. Make sure that you communicate about problems: You will run into problems when you work on databases. It is usually far better to take initiative to communicate with your customer about the problems than to avoid them.

3. Remember, you are looking out for the good of your customer: You do what is best for your customer even though it causes you some difficulty.

A number of years ago, I hired a contractor to work on a FoxBase Mac application for a customer who wanted to manage energy resources. I was the point of contact for the customer and my contractor assured me that they could do the work. After several weeks, it was obvious that we were not meeting the customer's needs. It was a combination of a lack of ability of my contractor plus changing requirements, plus the idiosyncrasies of FoxBase for the Mac. I finally found a reputable FoxBase provider and found that they were willing and able to do the work. I then met with the customer and told him that we could not complete the work and referred him to the other provider. He was not happy. But, I'm convinced it was the right thing to do. We, obviously, did not charge him for the work that we did not complete, even though I still had to pay the contractor. My only problem was that I took too long to make this decision.

Make sure that you face reality and help others face reality. This sounds simplistic, but your project will fail if your goal in the interview process is to please other people instead of honestly looking at the work they need to accomplish. You certainly want to be cordial and positive. But you must avoid expediency in the short run that will crash your work in the long run.

Make sure that you do not take criticism personally. People will criticize you. It is far better to receive the criticism in the beginning of a project than at the end. It is far better to be criticized for being too demanding about agreement on purpose in the beginning than to realize too late that you are working on a database in a situation where the purpose is always changing and you cannot meet the customer need.

Now that you have a realistic attitude, you are ready to get to work. Let's first discuss the steps you need to take to carry out the specification planning phase of our database development Blueprint.

Steps to Take for Gathering Specifications

Here are basic steps to following in gathering specifications.

1. Set up your team: Find the people that you need to work with.
2. Understand from the team what work needs to be done: Talk with the team to understand what work your database will do for the organization (work accomplishment perspective) and who will do what.
3. Decide on the database development needed to accomplish the work: Work out the database features you will build to accomplish the work objective (development perspective).
4. Create the Proposal: Create the document that lays out the specific work that you will do to build the database.
5. Obtain approval for the Proposal: This is a simple but very important step.

Don't forget that that this book takes you through an entire blueprint that covers most aspects of database development. The five steps mentioned above give you details on how to carry out the first phase of your Blueprint; the laying out specifications phase. Throughout the book, we will balance the big picture (what is going on with the Blueprint parts) with specific details on how to practically carry out the requirements communicated in each part of the Blueprint. Now, let's look at each of these specification planning categories in more detail.

Set Up Your Team

In this step, you identify the people who need to work with you on the database project. Notice that you will primarily use relational skills at this point rather than technical skills. As you follow the Blueprint, it is critical to work well with the people involved in your project. You need to constantly make the transition between focusing on the technical work and focusing on the relational dynamics as you work through the Blueprint. You must identify the people who will work with you on the project. If you take care to relate well with these people, it will help you greatly in carrying out your work. You might also find that you don't want to take on a project if you have difficulty identifying your team.

You have four basic groups of people that you need to consider in identifying your team:

1. Decision Makers (also normally called the Client)
2. Users
3. Developers
4. Technical Support Personnel.

Let's look at each group one at a time to determine who they are and how you will work with them.

Decision Makers

They are called **decision makers** because they are the ones who make decisions for the company.

> *The decision makers are the people who approve your work and ultimately benefit from your work.*

Other people may gather information and administrate policy; but the decision maker can take action on that information to make a binding judgment for the company. They are the ones who probably approve you working on the project. They are the ones who ultimately accept your work and approve your pay (if you are working as a contractor). They can also play an important role in making sure that people use the database you create. They benefit from your work because you save their business or organization time, money and/or you improve the quality of the organization.

It is important to do everything possible to give the decision maker what they want. For example, a department in an energy organization wanted to track new recruit training assignments. The decision maker wanted to see a bar chart showing the time frame for each employee and where they were working. This report helped her see the status of the workers at a glance and allowed her to plan and make decisions regarding future placement. The data about the employees was stored in an Access database. However, some of the data was recreated in Excel to produce a bar chart. This creation of the bar chart took several hours to produce and maintain. Also, the data was not always accurate because people kept the data in two places. A developer (myself) used the existing Access data and exported the proper data into Microsoft Project (since Microsoft Project's data is stored in four Excel spreadsheets) to create the same bar chart (thus avoiding the need to use Excel). He also wrote code in Microsoft Project and in their current Access application to automate the process. The report looked essentially the same and instead of taking several hours to produce, the report took about one minute to run and print. The decision maker was happy because she saved time and the automated method was more accurate. This project was a success because the decision maker got the results she was looking for. Also, the workers were happy because it saved them hours of time.

It is important that you figure out early in the analysis process who is your decision maker. They may or may not be the ones who contact you about developing a database. Even though the decision maker often does not play an active role in working with you, you need to consider them and make sure they support your work. Usually if you make the decision maker happy, you have completed a successful project.

In the same token, your project can go awry if you ignore this step. For example, several years ago a lawyer contacted me about setting up a database to store information used to build legal documents. I knew the lawyer and was happy to work with him because he was intelligent and knowledgeable about computer functionality. Several days into the project, the senior partner wanted to learn about my work. I met with him and explained the work and referred him to a prototype that I had developed. Over the next couple of weeks, I met with the senior partner to explain what I was doing because he was not as computer literate as my original contact. After three lengthy meetings, he still did not grasp how the entire system worked. Despite his lack of understanding, he began running the project. I asked him to approve the database design that we wanted to use in order to build the word processing documents. He would not approve the design. Instead, he kept changing the project requirements. Finally, I had to give up the work without getting paid. I had failed to consider this decision maker when setting up the project and it cost me. I wrongly assumed that the project would go well because of the knowledge and ability of my initial contact.

You find out who the decision maker is by asking and observing. When contacted about creating a database, ask who will give the final approval for the work. Another way to find out this information is to ask who approves payments. You can also look at published organizational information to see who is in charge of the area that wants you to do the database development. Make your best guess at who the key person is for your project and write down that person's name as one of your project assumptions (this topic is presented later). For example, you would write as an assumption: "I assume that Mr. Richards will be the point of contact for giving approval to the work."

Users

Users are important because they need to be able to use what you produce. If you are automating a manual system or improving productivity by developing a new system, they are good sources of information on how the work is currently being done. Or, you can observe them to determine how you can improve the work that they are currently doing. Decision makers are absolutely critical in your database development effort. However, if users decide they do not like your system, they can seriously impede your efforts by basically not using your database. It is possible that they can cause such a negative situation, that the decision maker (perhaps wrongly) is forced to side with the users, thus shutting down your project.

You have to win over the users to your new system if you want to successfully roll out your database. In order to do this, you want to work with users in four different ways:

1. Ask them HOW? Talk with them about how they currently do the work. You can then use these discussions as a basis for setting up your database.

2. Have them TEST: Have them test your work as you develop it. Since they will use your database, they will be the best judges of how your system works; if it really accomplishes what it needs to accomplish. You need to make sure they understand how to easily use your system. If users cannot understand your system during testing, you need to change it.

3. WIN them OVER: Communicate with users. If it is a system that is often used, you need to consider a public relations campaign geared toward the users. Sometimes you have to sell change. Many users tend to resist change. Any change management training you might have had should be applied here.

4. TRAIN them: Provide training for users. Depending on your expertise, it can take a great deal of work to "bullet proof" your application (set it up so that it will not crash) and still make it flexible. We will discuss how to achieve this goal in a later chapter. By teaching the users, you can tell them exactly how you want them to work with your application. This can save you development time by not having to spend as much programming time trying to anticipate user actions that you do not expect. Also, if you train users, they will have more confidence in the database and will be more likely to use it and use it well.

The users are an important group for you to consider. You should include them in initial discussions about understanding the work. They often perform the work, so they will understand the details better than the decision makers. You can obtain from them pertinent details to help you build the database such as: current paper forms, reports, answers to questions you have. Users are critical for testing your database. They provide excellent feedback on whether or not the database you are building does what it supposed to do. Also, they can give you feedback on the usability of the database. If they do not understand how to use it, chances are other users will not understand how to use it. You also need to consider users when making plans to **Roll out** your database.

> To Roll out your database means to install the final version so that everyone actually uses it to do their database work instead of whatever other method they were using. As part of the Roll out, you normally include special publicity and training activities to prepare users for this action.

Do not forget that people tend to resist change. The more you actively communicate with your users and inform them about the change and how it will accomplish the organizational mission and be beneficial to them personally, the better the roll out will go. Finally, train your users. If the users receive training they will more likely embrace the new database as a friend rather than as a threat. It will also minimize the anger they might feel towards you (the developer) by not knowing what to do. Training insures that people will know how to use the database that you create.

Developers

The next group that you want to consider when setting up your specifications is developers. In many small projects, you are the developer. You will actually build the database that you design. In larger projects, you may need other developers, especially if you have made a buy decision and hired another company to carry out the development and/or install and configure their commercial application (as needed). In these cases, you need to make sure that you think about how many other developers you need to complete the specifications that you establish. The key point in working with other developers is that you need to communicate the business requirements clearly to them and keep on communicating the business requirements clearly. Developers tend to focus on the details of their database development and can easily miss the purpose behind the work. The other developers may not hear you communicate with the decision makers and users to define the work requirements of the organization. So, you will serve as the primary person to interpret the business requirements to the other developers. You play a very important role. You are distinctive because you can work with users and decision makers in defining their requirements and you know how to communicate with developers. You normally include the developers after you fully define the database project. They implement the specifications that you present.

When working with developers, you need to communicate what standards you require (see section about standards later in the book). The larger the project, the more crucial it is for you to abide by database standards. You need to communicate these standards to your developers before the project begins.

Once the work begins, you need to communicate regularly with your developers about how they are doing and to make sure they understand the business purpose of their work. You also need to check their work. For the first week of the development work, you should consider performing these checks on a daily or every other day basis. This may slow down the work, but it is important that you identify developer problems early. The biggest problem you will uncover with developers will probably not be in the details of the code but in the end result. For example, a developer may build a form that pops up quickly with a beautiful picture. When the user clicks, this action calls code that brings up a video viewer that plays a file showing a lovely beach scene with breeze sounds. These things work. They are created correctly so don't crash. However, they do not accomplish the business purpose. You need to make sure that developers do not pursue the side roads of interesting technical issues, instead of the main highway of business usefulness.

Technical Support Personnel

The **Technical Support personnel** are important in a network situation.

> *Technical Support personnel are the people from the IS group who will install your database on the network and make sure the right people can access it.*

You need to identify a technical support person as part of your team. This person will serve as your point of contact for any technical support requirements. Normally, the decision makers will give you the name of this person. It is not imperative that the technical support person attend all of your meetings. However, they need to be available and responsive to your questions and requirements.

Technical support personnel are important because they understand the network and where things are on the network. You need them for three major reasons:

1. They know where to find the data.
2. They can install the application in the proper place on the network and make sure users access properly.
3. They control security.

Your technical support contact will help you mainly at the beginning of your database development and at the end of your development process. As you begin setting up your data structures (physical design) for your database, it is important to determine if some of the data that you need for your database is already available in the organization. This may be difficult to determine in larger organizations that are growing rapidly. However, in many cases your users can confirm that they are using data that you may want to include in your database. The challenge is finding out where the data is kept on the network and making sure that you can gain access to it. You do not want to reenter data that is already available in the organization. The technical support personnel can help you locate and use data that already exists. Having a technical support contact as part of your team will save you time and effort in building your database.

When you finish your database development and are ready to make your application available to your users, the technical support personnel can help again. They can help you install your database so it is available to the right people. This is particularly important if the people who will use your database are located on different servers or domains on the network, or if you will host the database on the Internet. They can also give you proper file paths for attaching other data so the attachment drives are not letter specific.

Finally, technical support personnel can help you with security. Many times, you will only want certain people to have access to certain functionalities in the database that you develop. The technical support personnel can set up your security on a certain drive or file.

Clarifying who will serve on your database development team is very important. Picking the right people will save you time and effort in providing a solution that will work well for everyone involved. Now you are ready to work with your team.

Decide on the Database Development Needed to Accomplish the Work

Now you change from the role of information gatherer to translator. You are ready to translate the business information into database information. You need to determine which database pieces you need to give you the business result that you desire. You might say that it is like the game of

Jeopardy. You receive the information about the organization in the form of a statement: "register students." Your answer (in the form of a question) is: "What does the *Registration* form, which is based on the *Registration* table pulling pick lists from the *Student* and *Schedule* tables, allow you to do?" *Register students* is the work goal that you discussed in your meeting that you want the computer to accomplish for you. The *Registration* form is the database **object** that will accomplish the business result.

> *An object is simply something that you work with when doing database development (for example; table, field, form …).*

As a *translator* you need to decide what data is required and how to combine that data in the proper format that will allow the users to do the required work.

This step of the design process is perhaps both the easiest and the most difficult one to do. It is easy in that it does not take too much time to create the database objects. It is difficult because it is totally flexible as to how you approach the design. There are usually many different ways to accomplish the business objective. The most important point to remember in this step of working out the database features is to only build database objects that will result in the business functionality that you know to be true. Do not speculate at this point. Give your customers what they ask for, not necessarily what you think they need (however, you may make suggestions).

Now comes the difficult part; you need to decide exactly what database objects you will produce and how long it will take to produce them. At this point, you may not be able to sketch out in exact detail what you will include in each database object. However, you need to state clearly which objects you will need. For example, suppose that you are building a case tracking system for a law firm. Based on your discussions with your customer, you know that you need the following functionality:

- Add, edit, and delete case information
- The cases occur for the same group of customers
- Archive old cases and be able to recall if needed

- Track payments made on cases to outside counsel
- Make reports on number of open cases, number of cases settled, total amount paid to outside counsel to settle a case.

You translate this business functionality into database objects. You know that you need the following database objects:

- Tables for Cases, Archived Cases, Customers, and Invoices. You also may need some pick list tables for data entry purposes.
- Forms for Cases, Customers, and Invoices. The Invoice form will be associated with a case, so the Case form will be complex.
- Reports on the number of open cases, the number of cases settled, and the total amount paid to outside counsel to settle.

By totaling up the number of objects, you can estimate the work required to build the database. In this case you have to build:

- Three tables (the archive table is simply a copy of the *Case* table so takes no time)
- Three forms (Invoice form will be a subform)
- Three reports.

The act of determining the number of objects needed per business requirement is an art. It takes experience to do it well. The rest of the book describes in detail how to build and use database objects. As you understand how to build specific database objects, you will obtain a better idea of which object will meet your business requirement. The rest of the Blueprint will give you the expertise that you need to match objects with requirements.

As you can see, this step of developing database features is both easy and difficult. It is easy in that you can write up the database requirements in a few pages of text. Determining these requirements based on business objectives takes mastering the rest of the parts of the database Blueprint.

Now it is time to pull all of your information together into a proposal and project schedule. Sometimes the proposal is called a Systems Design, Systems Profile, Systems Analysis document, or a Software Development Plan. It is more helpful to call it a *proposal* because it focuses the attention on doing the work to satisfy a customer (even though this customer may be internal to the organization) rather than a bureaucratic activity. Also, you want to secure approval for the proposal so you lock in the scope (see below) of the work. You propose to create a database to meet the stated business needs of your customer. Let's discuss how to draw up this document.

Create the Proposal

In this section, you will gain an understanding of what to include in the proposal. You will learn how to lay out your project and make time estimates. Particular attention will be given to scope definition.

The **proposal** serves as the guideline for the work that you will do for your customer (internally or externally).

> *The proposal is simply the document that you create that includes details what you discovered in the two steps: talk with your team and work out the database features.*

It is important for two reasons:

1. It serves as your guide for doing the work to make sure that you focus on what you agreed to do for the customer and do not go off on tangents.
2. It clarifies exactly what you will do for the customer (and what you will not do) so that there is agreement before you begin the work (not after).

If your customer is paying you directly for the work, this proposal serves as your time estimate for the project. It also allows you to decide when to invoice for your work.

If you are working on a large project, you will often find separate proposals written for each of the parts including, for example: data administration, user interface design, reporting, infra structure, rolling out the application, and training. You will probably work on only a piece of this larger job. You need to write a proposal for that piece of the project. That proposal will closely reflect the topics of the sections mentioned below but will go into much greater detail.

There are many ways to draft proposals. However, a good proposal will contain a title and four basic sections:

1. Overview
2. Business situation
3. Database requirements
4. Project plan.

Overview

In the title; include the name of the project, the company or department, the date, and a list of your planning team. The Overview section gives a brief summary about the organization and what the database will accomplish. You should answer the question; what events led up to the decision to create a database at this time? Give some background on what has happened in the past. Summarize what the members of the organization have said about their reasons for doing the database. Detail is not important here. It is more important to briefly give the overall picture.

Business Situation

In the business situation section, you summarize the information that you discovered in your meetings with the business personnel. You also identify by name any paper information (i.e. about reports they use or forms that have been filled out) that people gave you. Your customers should be able to read this section of the proposal and nod their heads in agreement that this is a correct summary of their work situation. The business situation section of the proposal contains the following topics:

- Goal: What do you want this database to do for the organization?
- Business needs: What are the particular tasks that you want this database to help you with?
- Business rules: What are the business rules that you want to follow with this database?
- Information Issues:
  o Inputs: What business information do you need to enter, maintain, and search for?

       o   Outputs: What business information to you need to output in the form of reports or screen summaries?

       o   Hardware: What hardware standards are in place for the organization?

       o   Security: What level of security do you require for the system?

- People:
  - Project Team: People who will work with you on this project and what role they will play.
  - Users: Who will use the system and how many?
  - Support personnel: Who will help with the network setup or retrieve data that is already out there?
  - Others in the Organization: People who have data that you might want to use and/or people who might want to use your data.

In the business goal statement, crystallize what business objective your customer will accomplish by using this database that you will build. For example, suppose you are a social worker compiling survey results. You want to create a database solution for your own company. You call this database the *Survey Tracking System*. Your goal for the organization is to quickly and accurately track survey results so that you can analyze the data for making effective decisions concerning our outreach programs to our customers. Your goal statement should reflect the purpose statement of your organization. In other words, this database should help your organization better achieve its purpose. If the database does not help your organization move toward its purpose, then why do it? But you also may want to use one of the readily available commercial products that can help you carry out surveys and just make sure (as we discussed earlier in the book) that you have access to the data containing the survey results so you can use for further analysis if needed.

In the business needs section, lay out your objectives in detail. Be specific on what you want to accomplish. Let's continue the social worker example. You want the Survey Tracking System to fulfill the following business requirements:

- The computerized system should look like the current paper survey.
- Make it quick and easy for clerical personnel to enter the survey results. For people taking the survey in the building, allow them to fill out the survey on-line.
- Be able to pull up the totals for each question.
- Graph the results of each question by percent.
- Graph the results of each question by work discipline.

Distribute the survey again in six months and run a statistical comparison between the original results and the new results.

In this section, it is important to include all of the items that you want to accomplish. However, do not worry too much about the details of how you will accomplish each need. For example, in the above example you did not explain how you would carry out the statistical analysis. This detail comes in the database requirements section.

The rest of the steps in the Business Situation section of the proposal are simply summaries of what you gleaned from the people in the organization when you conducted your information gathering.

Database Requirements

In this section, you want to write out how you will translate the business requirements into specific database objects.

You want to list the objects that you will need to create by category. You should include the following categories:

- Tables
- Queries and Reports
- Forms to capture data
- Forms to run the application
- Code to tie the application together
- Implementation.

These categories parallel the Blueprint that we follow in the rest of the book. Note how database work is a growing process for you. You learn this basic approach for creating your database requirements and then you learn many of the particulars needed to help you build a complete application. Understanding the particulars helps you understand what database requirements you need for the next project.

Begin your proposal with the tables (data design). Chapter 3 will focus on this topic in detail. In the proposal, simply list the tables that you need to include. The tables should reflect the people, things, and activities (also called *entities*) that you are tracking in the company.

Keep in mind that there are times when you should continue to use your manual data and not try to replace them with tables. For example, suppose you are building a database for a small business who wants to include the Dunn and Bradstreet number in their customer table. Because of the small number of customers involved, you should simply look up the Duns (data universal numbering system) number (on the Internet or purchased list) when needed instead of trying to create a lookup table of all companies who have a Duns number.

Also include tables that you use as pick lists for data entry purposes. These tables are also called **Lookup tables**.

> *A Lookup table is a table that exists for data entry purposes. This limited number of options is also called a domain or range of options.*

Instead of typing in a value to update a certain field, you can pick from a list of options. This allows you to limit the options that a user can enter into that field. The data in lookup tables does not change as often as regular tables. They exist to make data entry easier and more accurate. Many times, you want to put people or other things in your business into categories. For example, a person who takes a training class can fall into several categories: Employee, Contractor, or Special Student. You want to create a pick list table called *StudentCategory* which allows you to keep track of these categories.

If you will be using tables that are already present within the organization (i.e. in a commercial application), mention the tables that you will use, where they are located, who can give you access to them, and how you will use them (importing versus linking). Even though the tables already exist, it will take time for you to incorporate them into your database. Make sure that you make time estimates based on how long it will take you to secure these items.

In this section of your proposal, mention the exact number of tables that you will need to meet the objectives stated in the previous section. Count and list all three kinds of tables:

1. Main tables that reflect the people, things, and actions of your business
2. Pick list tables
3. Tables that you will use from other places, either by linking or importing.

Next, list the queries and reports that you need. Chapter 4 will focus on this topic in detail. The queries should pull out the sets of data that you need to show in your reports and forms. As much as possible, set up the queries before building the other database objects. This will make it easier for you to have the proper data to show in your reports and forms. You will use Action queries to manipulate data. Action queries change data so are useful for, among other things, archiving data; copying data that is no longer current from the main database file into another database file. This other database holds this "old" data so that you can get to it if you ever need it. This is useful because you have a record of activity in your database if you ever have a question about old data. Also, it allows you to build trend reports based on activity over a long period of time. Action queries are also used for data cleanup, something to be discussed later.

List the forms that you need to capture data. These are the forms that display data and allow you to work with your data. Working with your data includes adding, editing, and locating data. You will cover this topic in Chapter Six. List each form and give a description of what the form will do. Place any special instructions in this description. The description will also point out the data source and the sort order for the form. This forms section will reflect the needs that you highlight in the Business Situation section of your Proposal under Information Issues – Inputs. Count a subform (a form contained in another form and linked to the main form by a common field) as a separate form in your listing.

Now list the forms to run the application. You will cover this topic in detail in Chapter 6. These forms include **switchboards** and any other forms that are required to direct the user through the application.

A switchboard is like a menu on a form. It provides buttons that the user will push to take them to different parts of the database.

Other forms give messages, allow entry of variable information like date ranges, or allow users to set preferences. These forms are distinctive in that they do not have any data source. Forms are the way you normally build applications in Access. List all the forms that will help you move your users through their data and their needed outputs. Keep in mind that more and more, all functionality is built into the forms that display data and menu options versus switchboards.

List the reports in this section as well. The reports listed will reflect the needs that you highlight in the business situation section of your proposal under Information Issues – Outputs. You will have three basic kinds of reports:

1. Detail reports that give listings: This type of report can also include subtotals and grand totals. It can be a form of information that gives details about a particular piece of data. This type of report is often used for day to day information needs like: invoicing, printing certificates of completion for an educational course, or providing a list of overdue books for a library. Label reports are considered detail reports.

2. Summary reports that give totals: This type of report gives totals without giving the details. This type of report is used to provide an overview of how things are going. Examples of summary reports include: number of classes taught last month, number of copies of books on hand, amount of sales for the 4th quarter.

3. Charts give a visual representative of the data: This type of report is a special kind of summary report. It is useful for communicating trends, percentages, or comparisons. Keep in mind that it may be easier to bring data into Excel for charting.

Your next section will include your code. Simply indicate the places in Access where you will include code. This includes the forms, modules (discussed later), and reports (objects). Briefly describe the actions that will be accomplished in the object. This information will be covered in more detail in chapter 7. If you do reference any outside libraries (covered later in the book), indicate them here.

Notice that as you create this proposal that you are also creating the **documentation** for the system.

Documentation is a written explanation of what you did.

Documentation clarifies what you as a developer created and how people can work with what you created. This will help you after you finish when you have to support the work. You will have a guideline as to where to go to fix problems or add functionality.

Taking time to spell out your plan will focus your development. This will save you valuable time and help you communicate. You have clear direction. You will have direction in your work and will not go off on tangents.

Project Plan

Now you want to develop the project plan. As you do this, it is important to understand a little about **project management**.

> *Project management is the process of planning, describing, and tracking a job so that the work is completed on time and close to the budget.*

A project is a specific piece of work that has a definite starting time and a definite finish point. Project management is used widely in the construction business. You start building a bridge and eventually you complete it. To build the bridge, you need to take certain steps. You have to take these steps in a certain order. You need to prepare the supporting structures of the bridge before you add the road across the water. Before both of these activities, you need to obtain some good engineering studies to decide how high to build the bridge and what weight the bridge needs to support.

Project management is an entire course of study in itself. If you are interested in doing database development, you will do well to learn project management principles, tools, and techniques. Having project management expertise will set you apart as an excellent worker in the database development field. With project management skills, you will be able to make a realistic plan, track progress, and communicate clearly with your customer. This will make your customer very happy. Project management helps you and your customer face reality. In this section, we will look at a few key project management principles that will help you complete your Proposal.

First, let us look at some terms that you need to know. The key terms that you need to know are: *task, duration, work, milestone, scope, assumption,*

Let's take them one at a time, starting with **task**.

> *A task is one specific piece of work that you do to help you complete your job.*

For example, *create reports* is a specific piece of work that you need to complete. Completing this piece will move you forward in finishing the entire project of building a database. Suppose your project is to eat your dinner. You sit at the table. You take the knife and fork. You cut the succulent meat. You take a bite of juicy steak, cooked perfectly. Taking a bite of steak is one thing you do to help you eat your dinner. This bite of steak is the task. You might say that a task is a bite of the entire project. Once you have taken all the bites, you have eaten the meal; or finished the job.

You need to know the difference between **work** (also called effort) and duration.

> *Work is the actual time you spend on a task.*

Duration is different.

> *Duration is the amount of calendar time you take to complete that task.*

For example, suppose you are creating forms for your database. It takes you four hours of actual work to complete this task. However, you do not spend all of your time on this task. You have to teach a two-day database class, carry out two meetings for a different project, and take your daughter to the doctor. Even though you start working on the forms on Thursday morning, you do not finish the forms until Tuesday afternoon. The duration of the task is four days (weekends do not count). The point is that when you make time estimates, you make them according to the work required, but schedule the delivery dates according to the duration required. So, you charge your customer for four hours of work on the forms, but you tell your customer that you will deliver the forms on Tuesday afternoon.

As you plan your project, highlight the key tasks that you have to accomplish. These key tasks are called **milestones**.

> *A milestone is a distinctive task of zero duration that indicates an important accomplishment in the project.*

Normally, milestones are points in the project where you deliver something to the customer. Here are some examples of tasks that you should define as milestones:

- Deliver data design
- Deliver prototype of forms
- Obtain approval for reports
- Deliver full prototype
- Install final version.

It is good to define several milestones throughout the project to indicate progress and encourage accountability. Successful projects build in regular checkpoints in the project. These checkpoints provide for the work of the developers to make sure that they do not wander too far from the agreed-upon business requirements. Milestones serve as these checkpoints. They are helpful for the developers because they are points in the project where the customer must give approval. The developer can then move to the next part of the project knowing that the previous part is acceptable.

If you charge for your work, milestones are good places to submit your invoices for payment. If you charge for database development, make sure that you spread out your invoices. Do not wait until the project is complete before you ask for payment. Match your payment requests to two or three of your milestones. For example, when you deliver the database design you can ask for payment for the hours you have worked up to that point.

Scope is absolutely critical as you lay out your project plan.

> *Scope is describing exactly what you will produce or perform in the project and what you will not produce or perform.*

The idea in determining scope is to get into the head of your customer and determine what they expect. Customer expectations that agree with the goals of the development are listed under scope as things that you will accomplish. As you consider the thinking of your customer, you must also uncover expectations that do not reflect the agreed-upon goals of the project. These false expectations are listed under scope as things that you will not accomplish. Here are some examples of several scope statements:

- Create 8 tables with Relationships defined
- Create 12 forms per the definition from the proposal
- Will not include Internet capabilities
- Will not provide user documentation
- Will not deploy application on company servers (or cloud).

You get the picture. Scope clarifies expectations. Proper scope definition is the key to helping developers and customers work well together. Whether you make or buy, scope needs to be clearly stated.

Perhaps the best way to manage expectations regarding scope is to carry out your development in **phases**.

> *A phase is a development project that meets customer desires for productivity but does not necessarily satisfy all of their desires.*

For example, suppose you want students to register for classes. The desire of the customer is for students to register individually over the Internet. It can be expensive and time consuming to set up and secure an entire student registration system over the Internet that is user-friendly, secure, and accurate. The customer may not have the money or hardware infrastructure or personnel to accomplish this desire. You might not have the time or expertise to accomplish it.

A better solution in many cases is to break up your development effort into phases. Phase I involves setting up a student registration system on a network used by a small workgroup. People can call in their class request and the administrator can enter the information into the local application. You can pull accurate and timely reports from this data. Notice that Phase I gives you definite gains in productivity. One person can manage the database while taking phone calls. Phase 1 allows you to try out the database and make changes as required.

You will put the database on the Internet during Phase 2. Notice the focus on productivity. You gain immediate productivity by developing a workgroup solution to your scheduling requirement. While you are productive with Phase 1, you can develop Phase 2. When you complete Phase 2, you can bring your data into the new version.

As a rule of thumb, you normally gain approximately 80% of your productivity in 40% of your development time. What you want to do is complete enough development so that there is a maximum productivity gain. Make this development effort Phase 1.

Many times, organizations do not have a clear idea of all that they want a database to do. They spend a great deal of time analyzing all the possibilities. This is good to a point. However, many times they are clear on a few major things that they want the database to do. Instead of worrying about all of the possibilities, in many cases they should build a database to accomplish their current, clear objectives (Phase 1). If the data design is done well, other features can be added later (Phase 2). Also, note that the milestones often come at the end of phases.

Along with scope, it is important to state your **assumptions**.

Assumptions are events that you believe must happen if your project will finish on schedule.

You clarify assumptions to control expectations. You make time estimates based on events happening a certain way. So, if one of your assumptions does not hold true, then your time estimate does not hold true. If your time estimate does not hold true, you have a reason (or at least an explanation) for not staying on schedule.

Make assumptions about equipment, personnel, and change requests. Here are some examples of project assumptions:

- We assume that the user will have the Windows 10 Pro 64-bit operating system and Access 2016.
- We assume that the two people of the database team who are designated to test the database work will be available at least 25% of their time on the two days designated on the project schedule.
- We assume that only one person will be the point of contact for changes.

Your project schedule will reflect the size of the project. For example, a small project is one that fits the following criteria:

- Takes approximately 40 hours or less to complete.
- Is completed by one or two people.
- Affects a workgroup or small company (approximately one to ten people).

Keep in mind that the principles you learn will also apply to larger projects. Because you are learning a holistic approach to database development in this book, we are focusing on smaller projects for our model. Now you are ready to make your time estimates.

It is important to make time estimates of how long you will take to complete the work that you agree to do in your proposal. You also want to obtain estimates for any outside company that you have hired and make sure they are realistic. Estimating time is an art. Each person works differently. Some of you will work more quickly than others. The automobile repair industry has a book that tells you how long it takes to create something to carry out certain repairs on your car. For example, the book may say that it takes 1.5 hours to perform a brake job. Some mechanics may complete the work faster than 1.5 hours and some will take longer than 1.5 hours but the estimate is 1.5 hours. There is nothing like this in Access. The main reason why is that every database is different. Every form that you design is not the same. This is unlike an automobile where brake jobs for 2016 Camry's will basically be the same. However, by understanding some basics about time estimation, you can begin to build a project plan that is realistic.

There are several ways to determine how long you will take to do something in Access. I will give you three basic techniques and then give you a couple examples of specific estimates that I use.

Time Estimate Technique #1 - Past experience. Past experience is the best way to determine how long something will take in the future. If you have done something similar, you can better estimate how long it will take you to do similar work. Whenever you work on a project, make it a point to keep a log of how long it takes you to actually do the work. Make sure you include the actual time you are involved in the work (in Project Management Terms, this is called duration) including time to stretch, to visit the rest room, and to pause for something to drink. Do not include the 15-minute conversation about the weather or the upcoming wedding. This habit of writing down time will give you a firm foundation for estimating future projects for now and in the future.

Time Estimate Technique #2: Talking with experts. Talking with experts is a good alternative to estimating work that you have not done yourself. Ask someone to tell you the number of hours needed to do a certain piece of work. One of the weaknesses of this technique is that you have to take time to explain generally what you will do on your project. This takes time and may make it difficult for the expert to make a realistic estimate. Also, the ability of the expert is reflected in the estimate. Experts take less time to do work than novices. They often use shortcuts that are not readily transferable to the novice. So, the time estimate from the expert may not work for you. Some database people are self-proclaimed experts but use techniques that are idiosyncratic and may not prove useful to you (or anyone else for that matter). Even though they complete work, no one can figure out what they did when they finish.

Another problem is that you may run into difficulty finding an actual expert who will take the time to work with you. If they are indeed experts, they may not have time to fit you into their busy schedules. You usually have to seek them out on their terms; like at user's group meeting or at special conferences. Despite these shortcomings however, talking with an expert is a good option.

Time Estimate Technique #3: PERT Technique. The Navy developed the PERT technique in the 1950s. **PERT** stands for *Program Evaluation and Review Technique.*

> *PERT is a visual way of showing how different tasks relate to one another.*

It is beyond the scope of this book to discuss this technique in detail. However, one aspect of the PERT approach was to introduce a method for making time estimates for tasks. People found that this method was useful in predicting the actual amount of work required. Here is how it works. You calculate the time based on three estimates. The three estimates include:

- Best case: How long it will take to do the work if everything goes perfectly.
- Worst case: How long it will take if you encounter maximum difficulty.
- Realistic: How much time you think it will actually take.

The formula reads as follows:

Work = (Best + Worst + (3 x Realistic)) divided by 5

Notice that you are giving more weight to the realistic scenario. So, if you are estimating the time to complete your forms, you can calculate the time needed as follows:

Best case = 3 hours
Worst case = 7 hours
Realistic case = 4
Estimated work = $(3 + 7 + (3 \times 4))/5 = (10 + 12)/5 = 22/5 = 4.4$ hours.

You can easily set up a spreadsheet to make this calculation. It is a good technique to use if you are able to obtain the feedback from several different experts. You can use the different estimates of the experts as your best case, worst case, and most realistic scenario. This method is also a good one to use if you are working on a team. Ask the team members for the three-time estimates suggested by the PERT technique. Take the highest, lowest, and average of the estimates from your team members. Apply the PERT calculation to these numbers. The result should give you a very good estimate.

Making time estimates can prove difficult. Each database project is different, so each one requires different functionality. You will run into two problems because of this difference in database projects. One is a lack of experience. Because you have no experience in building this different functionality, you do not know how long it will take you to complete a certain task in the current project. Even though you understand how to do it theoretically, you have never done it. Another is a lack of knowledge. Not only do you lack experience but you lack the knowledge of how to approach it. It may take you time to gain the knowledge to produce the database functionality you need.

For example, your customer wants you to produce a report showing the total and average hours worked per week for each worker. The report also needs to show the average overtime for each worker and the entire department for the week. You may know the concepts of how to produce a crosstab report, but you have not done it. You are confident that you can create this kind of report, but you just do not know how long it will take. You have difficulty estimating how long this report will take to produce because of a lack of experience. As you begin the work, you run into a problem. You find that the averages do not calculate properly. You receive error messages in the calculations and you have not run across this problem in your study or experience. You have to figure it out by using Access help and experimenting with different approaches or by going out and doing research or by talking to another expert to figure out the solution. You finally realize that it is a problem with nulls. In this case, you have difficulty estimating how long this report will take to produce because of a lack of knowledge.

Here are some additional rough guidelines to follow when making your time estimates. First of all, do not make estimates on a project when you do not have the information you need. At times, a customer will tell you their general goal for a database and ask you to tell them how long it will take. Your answer is: "I do not know exactly at this point how long this project will take, but let's approve 10 hours of time for me to get to work with the plan and design and then we will have a much clearer picture for estimating the rest of the project." The idea is to charge by the hour for any work you do until you have enough information to build a realistic plan. Once you have a plan, you can then make estimates of your hours and submit a **fixed-price bid**.

> *A fixed-price bid is a bid where you give one price for all the work that you do on a project. You must stick to the original bid for time and cost.*

Once you gather the information suggested by our Proposal, then you are ready to make some estimates. Here is a very rough guideline for estimates that I use. These estimates are per object (remember, an object is something you work with in Access like a table you design or a query you create):

- Table design: .5 hour per table (unless lookup table which takes little time)
- *Data Form design: 1 hour (for one-page forms, add approximately an hour per tab for tabbed forms)
- System Form design: 1 hour (includes attaching code, but not creating the code)
- Processing for a form: .5 hour for basic coding. More as needed.
- *Report design – basic: .5 hour
- *Report design – complex: 1 hour (subreports w/ calculations add .5 more).

(*Note: The estimates for forms and reports include the building of queries as needed to serve as the data source.)

Keep in mind that these time estimates include such things as backing up, testing the basic functionality of your work as you go, and application integration. So, make sure to add this time to your calculation.

Normally, you should not charge the customer for the time it takes you to learn a technique that you should know to fulfill the requirements. However, if they have an unusual request for functionality that requires you to develop a new technique, you should certainly charge for most if not all of this work. Use good judgment and be fair.

If the customer changes the scope of work or does not provide assumed items, you need to add additional time to the project. This is called a **change order**.

A change order is a document that describes work that you will do that adds to the original scope of the project and allows you to charge for these additional hours.

The customer must approve this change (by signing the document) before you proceed.

Once you have completed all of your other time estimates, you want to add some **contingency** time (5% to 15% or more depending on how clear or vague the job is).

A contingency is something unknown that will happen to increase the time required to finish the work.

To calculate contingency, you want to add up your time estimates for all of the work and then multiply it by a percent (from .05 to .15). Simply label it as *contingency* and add it to your previous total. This gives you your total time estimate for the project.

Now that you know the time estimates, you want to set up a schedule for when you will do the work. This is best accomplished by using a tool like Microsoft Project to show a visual depiction of the project schedule. Again, it is beyond the scope of this book to go into all of the details of project management. If you are buying the database service, you will want to review the project schedule of the vendor.

This is a very short task but a very important one. For smaller projects, you can have the decision maker simply take a copy of the proposal, write the word APPROVED, and then sign it and date it. Give the decision maker a copy and you keep a copy for your files.

Establish Application Development Standards

Now you have a great plan. This proposal will serve as a working model for all of the detailed parts that you will build. You are almost ready to get going on the work. Think of yourself as a drag racer. Your engine is revved. The Christmas tree light is flashing down to green. We have one more adjustment to make on your development hot rod before you peel out.

You are fulfilling your role as database leader. You can see how this masterpiece will look. You can see how it will benefit you and the rest of the team. Look at the happy nods. Visualize what you will do with that free time. Now you will add glue to the process by including solid **Database Development standards**.

> *A Database Development standard is an agreed-upon way of doing your work.*

Following standards is a form of communication between you, your users, other developers, and yourself. You want people to know where you are going with your work. Setting standards is like setting up rules of government for your development world. There are many ways to lay down standards. But like any form of government, it is important to maintain standards that really help and avoid picayune standards that are simply intrusive and in fact take more time to maintain than they save you in helpfulness. As an accomplished database leader, you should maintain database development standards in the following areas:

1. Naming conventions
2. Writing descriptions for objects
3. Structuring your Visual Basic for Applications (VBA) code.

Let's look at some minimum standards for Access database development. We will examine each of our three key areas for maintaining standards, explain why each one is important, and recommend specific ways to approach them in Microsoft Access.

Meet with the Team to Agree on Specifications

Insist that the team clarify what the business does BEFORE any meeting about database specifications. Hours of wasted time occur (including expensive fees to consultants) when a team comes together to discuss database specifications and they don't really know how their business works and why. A database is a tool not a "solution," They need to figure that out first, as the database simply reflects and automates how their business works. So, the team that meets to discuss the business may be different from the team that meets to discuss the database application.

Hopefully you will have a motivated, well-informed team to help lay out specifications. Like putting together any good team, give thought to who to include and make selections not just based on position! Keep the size to that required for a high-performance team (5-7). Don't forget the phases for forming an effective team (forming, storming, norming, performing) and that there may well be conflict in the early going. This actually is a good thing if handled well. Also, don't forget to use best practices and form a team covenant (hopefully the organization has done this already for teams) that sets the rules of behavior expected from the team and what happens if the covenant is not kept. Also, the Blueprint (whether for a commercial application or one that is designed) involves carrying out a project so take notes for each meeting and use project management best practices (beyond the scope of this book to discuss in detail but certainly project management principles are alluded to throughout). The purpose of the team is to benefit the organization so make sure the team understands what work your database will do for the organization (work accomplishment perspective). Now that you have defined the team that you will work with, you need to meet with the decision makers and users to establish the business requirements.

Set up the planning meeting. Ask the people who will come to bring reports that they currently produce, paper forms that capture information, computer files that they manipulate, and other questions that they need to answer about their work. It is important that they dig these items up before you formally meet with them. Make sure that you keep all of these documents in your files for future reference. It is also helpful to obtain some written statement of the purpose of the group. You want to find out exactly what they are currently doing and how that fits with the stated purpose of the organization.

As you meet with your customer, you have three goals that you want to accomplish:

1. Establish what they want this database that you will create to do for them.
2. Establish exactly how the group is currently carrying out this work (if any).
3. Confirm what resources you will have available.

Start the meeting by immediately stating your goals for the meeting. Continue with introductions. After the introductions, begin by asking; "What do you want this database to do for you?" Normally the decision maker will reply first. Write the answer down on a board (or somewhere else where everyone can see it). If appropriate, encourage others to respond. Summarize these answers in a short, concise manner. Make sure everyone agrees with the statement and that the statement reflects the organizational purpose.

You particularly want to know what questions they want to answer with this database system. For example, in an engineering bid-control system, they may want to know how many bids resulted in contracts within the last six months. They may also want to know; in the last year, with which type of business do we have the most final contracts? Sometimes, people simply want to be able to find information quickly. For example, a former student may call and ask: "which courses did I take in the fourth quarter of 2017"? Laying out the issues will help manage expectations.

The information that you obtain in this meeting will serve as your guideline for queries and reports. Be specific. Determining what information they want to pull out of the system will determine what data you want to capture. Ask them to list on a board exactly which reports they want. Ask for diagrams of how they want the information presented. For example, if they want a report on how many students complete training in a particular department, you want to know exactly which pieces of data will appear on the report, how it will be sorted, and any groups and calculations. It is much easier if they simply sketch out on a piece of paper how they want the report to look. This sketch commits them to that design. Make sure that they tell you the constraints they want to place on the data they want to report; such as a date range. This information will help you determine the query that will underlie the report. You also want to find out if they use information from some other part of the organization.

You now have clarified your overall purpose and some of the details of what you need to accomplish. Now you need to tie this information together in context to produce an overall picture of the work that needs to be done. You want to obtain a clear idea of what work currently happens, or what they want to happen. There are many techniques for carrying out this objective. The best approach is always to actually write out the flow on a board so that everyone in the group can see it. Include in your diagram people or other things involved, decision points, and other appropriate information. Keep a separate list of business rules. You also want to ask them about future developments. If you can create the resulting database in a way that allows for easy expansion to meet future requirements, this is good.

As part of this process, you might actually role play the process in the room. Have members of the team play the roles of the different parts of the process. Remember, you are trying to nail down the actual work in this initial discussion. The database development comes later.

For example, suppose you are developing a bid proposal system for an engineering firm. You might invite members of your team to play the roles of customer, sales person from your company, and the person who enters data. Have a copy of the customer specification form on hand at the meeting. Now you can have the *sales person* walking up to the *customer* and *interview* them. The *sales person* then *fills out* the customer specification form, leaves the *customer* and then walks across the room to deliver the *filled-out* form to the *data entry* person. You then might have an *engineer* creating a *proposal* that is *entered* into a database.

The idea in this entire process is to clarify exactly what happens. Role playing helps expose parts of the work flow that may not otherwise be identified. It also might provoke new ideas about how to do things better. For example, in the above example the decision maker might say he wants the sales people to enter the data directly rather than passing it off to a data entry person. Role playing also confirms the details that you discussed earlier and puts them in their work context. Take your time. Let the group figure out what is going on. Try to summarize events for them and direct the role play. Note all events on the board.

As an alternative to role playing, you can pick up a video camera and record the actual work process. This technique takes more time but is more realistic. You can have the real people describe what they are doing in the process, show forms they are working on, and analyze what they do. You now have a real record of the system instead of trying to recreate it. The other advantage of video-taping is that it begins to engender participation by others in the organization in this new project. This ethos will prove very useful later on in the Blueprint as you try to encourage people in the organization to use what you create.

There are also a couple of formal techniques for helping you understand the requirements. One technique is the interview technique. This approach involves more detailed interviews with various members of the organization to determine requirements. In interviewing, the goal is to obtain information from each person and also to ascertain feelings about the current system and potential changes. The benefits of this approach are:

- You involve many people in the analysis which helps them buy into what you are doing and thus facilitates change.
- You obtain a larger pool of information from which to form your opinion of the current situation, which should give you a more accurate picture.

The negative aspects of this approach are:

- It depends too heavily on the interviewer. He alone is responsible for directing the conversation and normally for sorting out the information received. This can skew the results.
- It takes too long because more people are involved. This can result in a greater expense because more people are pulled off of their work.

A variation of the interview technique is to send out surveys to many people that asks them about their work and what they might want in a new system. It also allows you to obtain feedback from people who may not work at the main location. Observation is another variation; simply watching what happens. This is good to a point, but also takes time to carry out.

The other formal technique is called JAD; which stands for *Joint Application Design*. This approach involves a group meeting where developers and users meet over a period of several days to discuss system requirements. It is reserved primarily for building large systems. The goal is to produce results similar to the interview system but to do this more efficiently. This results in a savings of time and resulting expense. JAD is simply a more formal version of the basic approach that we discussed earlier in this chapter.

At the end of your meeting, you need to make sure that you clarify who will do what in the project that will follow. You need to clarify the following roles:

- Who will give final approval for the work
- The two or more people who will serve as the test team for the project
- Your technical point of contact who will handle network and installation issues.

You also need to locate other data that might interface with this system. DO NOT make time estimates at this point. You do not know how long the work will take until you complete the all the steps.

You need to assemble all of the information that you obtained and organize it. Create a file folder for this purpose. Do this as soon after the meeting as possible. Ideally, you will use a laptop computer in the meeting to jot down notes. Make sure that you copy down any information that was written on the board. Add any paper forms, reports, or procedural instructions that you received. These notes will form the basis for the first part of your proposal.

Keep in mind that the larger the system, the less time you will spend on programming and the more time you will spend on defining the work. Your need for laying out specifications and communicating with people on your team will grow exponentially as the size of the work grows.

Naming Conventions

Now, let's look at naming conventions, using Access as our example. Database naming conventions (at minimum) will apply to:

- Main objects
- Fields in tables
- Controls on forms and reports
- Variables in VBA code.

Naming conventions are important because they serve as an "audit trail" to each part of your application. For example, Visual Basic development is chock full of objects. (NOTE: When I mention Visual Basic, I am referring to Visual Basic for Applications which works within Microsoft Office - VBA. Visual Basic is the stand-alone product. However, the two are similar in functionality. We will discuss VBA in more detail later in the book). The names allow Access to figure out which object you want to work with. Access (actually the person who programmed it) really does not care what you call an object. But, each object has to have a unique name. In fact, if you do not name your objects, Access will name them for you; memorable names like *Text22*. If you are going to work with an object, you want to give it a name that is meaningful to you.

Actually, clear and consistent naming is one of the secrets to doing solid database development. If you can organize yourself in this endeavor, you are well on your way to success. You want to name your database objects for three important reasons:

1. It will allow end users to understand the data elements they need to answer questions from the data through queries.
2. It will allow other people to figure out your application so that they can support it.
3. More importantly, it will allow you to figure out what you did.

When you create a solid database, other people in the organization will want to use your data. Normally, they will want to summarize the data for decision support type reports. For this reason, it is particularly important that you clearly name your tables and fields. This will make it easier for end users to find the data elements they need to answer the questions they have.

As you continue to succeed as a database developer, you will have other opportunities to build databases. You will dive into these projects. You will forget how your database works. Others may need to support the database that you create. You want to give them the opportunity to add to what you have created. By using clear and consistent names for your objects, you will quickly and easily find out where you need to make changes.

As you may recall from Genesis (Genesis 2:15-20), God gave Adam and Eve the charge to take care of His creation. God placed men and women as stewards over all of creation; and we must be good ones! One of the responsibilities of "ruling" was to name the animals. This was a tedious but important task. Database development is of a very different magnitude, but yet still similar to what was done. When you name your objects, you are giving order and meaning to your database creation. The names of your database objects should reflect the business world that your data describes. For example, you can call people that you provide service for: customers, clients, the insured, patrons, or fans. You choose your term depending on your purpose. Like in Creation, everything that you include in your database has a purpose. The name should remind you of that purpose.

There are many different ways to name database objects. If you perform database work for a company, ask them if they use any database standards. If the organization uses standards, using them will save you time and help you fit in with their way of doing things. If they do not have standards, they will be impressed that you asked. Maybe, you can even make an inside sale (as a consultant, this is a sale that you make of your services for additional work that follows from your original work) to develop a set of standards for them.

Throughout this chapter, we have emphasized a realistic approach to laying out your database plan as the first step in your Blueprint for success. Your plan is not an end in itself. Some of you will have a tendency to make the plan an end in itself. You tend to be very detailed. You are meticulous. You do not like to take risks. You may want to overdo the planning to the point that you delay finalizing the plan and implementing the plan. Others of you are very action oriented. You want to start hacking away immediately. You want to put out a working database yesterday. You do not want to bother with a plan. You may want to ignore planning to the point that you start working too soon before clarifying what you want to accomplish. You need to take more time to plan while keeping your urge to begin building.

These tendencies apply to establishing database standards. You want to have enough standards to gain the benefits of making support easier and saving you development time. You also want to save time by not naming objects unnecessarily. Each situation that you work in will differ. Just remember, as some have said; the name you give an object is a commitment to use that name; like giving a player a number or even naming our children.

Now, let's answer the question; "what objects do you name"? Access creates a plethora of objects. It is tedious to name all of these things. You want to compare the benefit gained from this naming process when you could be building your application. You may think that naming things is like spinning your tires in mud or treading water. You want to move forward but this naming activity does nothing but slow you down. It is better to think of it as putting caulk around your windows and insulation in your walls when building a house. It does not seem to make the house go up faster, but it sure cuts down on operating expenses and generally makes your house last longer. Caulking even cuts down on bugs and other wild life that might want to wander into your home.

Remember that when you work with Access, focus your naming conventions on the following areas:

- Main objects
- Fields in tables
- Controls on forms and reports
- Variables in VB code.

Let's look at some general principles surrounding the naming of objects, then we will look at the naming of the particular objects in the first three categories.

1. First of all, your object name should describe what the object represents. Also, avoid abbreviations. Spell out the term. We have made this point already. For example, the report *rptSalesYearEnd* is a report object (note prefix *rpt*) that gives the totals of sales for the entire year.
2. Secondly, your name should not include spaces or any special characters such as: ?, *, !, or /. If you do want to show a break in your name, use an underscore (_), not a dash (-).
3. Finally, your table and field names should be in the singular. For example, call your customer table; *customer*, not *customers*.

Note in Access, the object name is made up of three parts:

1. Optional prefix and suffix descriptors
2. An object type tag name
3. Object name.

The name looks like this:

[prefix]tagObjectName[suffix]

The tag (for everything except table and field names) and your object name are recommended. The prefix or suffix descriptors are optional (the brackets above indicate that they are optional). Put prefix object type tags in lower case. This makes it easier for your eye to take in the object name which is the main part of the object name.

The tag is three letters and identifies the type of object. This tag is helpful because it immediately tells you what type of object you are working with. For example, Access often presents you with a list of different data sources. This list includes tables and queries of different data sources. Without memorizing names, the only way to tell which items in the list are queries is to look for the prefix tag, *qry*.

The prefix descriptor further clarifies the function of your object. For example, it is helpful to know that *uqrySetDateSent* is an update query (note prefix *u*) that changes the *DateSent* field to today's date. You see a special update query icon next to the query name in the database window. But this visual reminder does not show up when you refer to the query in Visual Basic code. Adding the prefix to the name of the query makes it clear that the query is an update query.

The suffix descriptor works in a similar way. For example, *frmClassSub* is a subform showing students linked to *frmClass*.

Naming Main Objects

Now that we have looked at the general points to keep in mind when you name objects, let's examine the specific naming conventions you should use for each **main database object**.

> *Main database objects in Access are the ones that are listed on the tabs on the main Database Window of Access.*

The main database objects, with their tags, are:

> Tables: No tag on main tables. Names in lower case and singular.
> For lookup tables (optional), add prefix tag **ltbl**.
> For system tables (optional), add the prefix tag **stbl**.
> Queries: **qry**
> Forms: **frm**
> Reports: **rpt**
> Macros: **mcr**

Visual Basic Modules: **bas** (this stands for *Basic*, short for Visual Basic for Applications)

Notice that you have different categories of tables.

Lookup tables are helpful because they limit the domain (or set) of options a person can choose from when entering data. **System tables** help store constant values.

> *A System table is a table that contains information that you use in your database application.*

For example, you might want a company name to show on the footer of a report. Rather than hard coding a company name, you can refer to it in a System table. You might also want to store the locations of various files.

If you are testing any of these objects and you do not necessarily want to put them with your actual application, put a *zz* in front of the object name. For example, suppose you import a form called *frmSchedule* from which you will borrow code for your current database. After you import the form, you might rename it *zzfrmSchedule*. This sorts all of your test objects at the end of the list in your database window. This technique makes sure that you do not mingle the test form with your real form. If you create temporary objects in code, you should add a prefix descriptor of *zt*.

Use the following prefix descriptors with different types of queries:

> Append query: **a**
> Crosstab query: **c**
> Delete query: **b**

Make table query: **m**

Update query: **u**

Use the following prefix descriptors with different types of forms:

Lookup Form – a form that goes with a lookup table: **l**

Application Form – all forms that you use to run the database application except for Switchboards. You do not normally use this form to capture data that you will store in your tables: **a**.

Use the following suffix descriptors:

Subform or sub report: **sub**.

I recommend a couple of other conventions to use when naming particular main database objects.

1. First of all, if you are using a query as the data source for a form or report, tie the name of the query to the name of the form or report. For example, you create a report called *rptStudentsInCourses* that gives you the number of students taught in different courses for the semester. You should name the query that provides the data for this report *qryrptStudentsInCourses*. By using this technique, it becomes immediately clear that the query is tied to a particular report. This makes it easier to find and work with the query that you need to change for a particular form or report.

2. Secondly, tie the names of macro or Visual Basic module libraries (discussed later) to the forms or menus that call them. For example, you may have a switchboard form called *frmMainSwitchboard* that controls your application.

3. Thirdly, make your table names nouns with adjectives preceding. Always include a noun in the table name. The adjectives are optional. For example, you might have invoices in your database for customers (money that you will collect) and vendors (that you will pay). You should name the former *CustomerInvoice* and the latter

VendorInvoice. You could also name them respectively. It is possible to put both in the same table but that is another topic.

Naming Fields in Tables

Now you are ready to name your fields. Naming fields in tables does not require any clear-cut rules beyond the ones that apply to any object. However, you should use the following guidelines:

Keep names as short as possible without losing the meaning of the work items to which they refer. For example, if you want to keep track of social security number, name the field *SSN*.

Your field names should be exactly the same as the work items to which they refer. For example, lawyers often refer to cases as "matters." If so, make sure you name this field *MatterName*, not *CaseName*.

Fields (can also be called *columns*) in different tables that refer to exactly the same work item should have the same field name. For example, *MatterNumber* is a field that uniquely identifies each situation that a lawyer has to deal with. Each invoice applies to a particular matter, so you want to include the *MatterNumber* in the invoice table as a reference. Notice that you keep the field names exactly the same in the *Matter* table and in the *Invoice* table.

Except in the above situation, I suggest that you make each field name in a database unique. For example, you might have a field *LastName* that applies to your customer. You might also have the need for *LastName* in your *Consultant* table and in your *Vendor* table. I think it is easier to give each of them a unique field name. Call the last name field in the customer table *LastName*, in the consultant table *CustomerLastName*, and in the vendor table *VendorLastName* Keep in mind that a number of database developers may disagree with this recommendation. They suggest that you name all three fields *LastName* and distinguish them by adding the table name in front of the field name: *CustomerLastName*, *ConsultantLastName*, and *VendorLastName*. I think this approach can be confusing to end users and more time consuming for some developers. However, like all these recommendations, you should make your own decision about which technique you prefer. As mentioned above, the main thing is to have an approach.

Naming Controls on Forms and Reports

Now you are ready to name your **controls** on forms and report.

Controls are tools for form and report objects that allow you to show data, text or links to websites, graphics, or other files.

You place a control on a form or a report by using the Access Toolbox while in report or form design. Different controls from the Toolbox do different things. We will cover controls in more detail later in the book when we cover forms. When you place a control on a form or a report, Access gives it an arbitrary and meaningless name. If the control is bound (tied to a particular field so that when the form is in *View* mode it will display values stored in that field), Access gives the control the same name as the field. This can cause confusion in development as to what you want to refer to – the field or the control on the form. For these two reasons (and others), it is important that you name some controls.

The name of the control should follow the general conventions we have already covered. It is also fine to include the field name that is the data source for the control in the control name. I recommend that in addition to these conventions, that you include certain tags with your control names, depending on which type of control you use. The type of control and corresponding tag name to include as a prefix are:

Chart: **cht**
Check box: **chk**
Combo box: **cbo**
Button: **but**
Label: **lbl**
Line: **lin**
List box: **lst**
Option button: **opt**
Option group: **grp**
Page break: **brk**
Section : **sct**
Shape: **shp**

Subform or report: **sub**
Text box: **txt**
Toggle button: **tgl**.

Variables in VB Code

The last item to look at regarding our naming standards are **variables** in Visual Basic code.

A Variable is a temporary holder of information that needs a value that can change depending on the situation.

They are used in Visual Basic to refer to database objects (i.e. *fields*) or for other purposes to make your code easier to maintain and to make it easier to use with other applications.

Visual Basic uses many types of variables. You must make sure that the variable you define matches the type of information that you are storing in the variable. We will talk more about this later in the book when we discuss Visual Basic coding.

Use a tag when defining your variables. The tag indicates the type of data that the variable is storing. When using variables that refer to main database objects, simply use the tag that you normally use for that database object. For example, if you create a variable for a form, you can name that variable *frmMyForm*. Use the following tags when naming other variables in Visual Basic:

Workspace: **ws**
Database: **db**
Recordset: **rs**
Dynaset: **ds**
Snapshot: **snp**
Currency: **cur**
Single (number): **sng**
Double (number): **dbl**
Long (number): **lng**

Integer: **int**

Boolean (Yes or No): **bol**

String: **str**

Variant (any data): **var**

Control: **ctl.**

This list is not exhaustive but gives you the ones that you will use most often in Visual Basic coding. Don't worry if you do not recognize some of these names. As mentioned, we will cover them in a later chapter.

Writing Descriptions for Objects

Along with database development naming conventions, you should also provide **Object descriptions** for your main database objects and for fields.

An Object description in the Access database world is a particular property for an object where you can simply explain what the thing is and does.

Descriptions clarify exactly what business item the object refers to or what the object does in the database. The name of the object (what we just discussed) gives you some clue as to the business meaning of the database object. However, the description can give you much more detail. Adding descriptions also prepares you for printing technical documentation for your work. Remember, you are trying to keep track of what you are doing so that you and everyone else remembers exactly what work your database is referring to. Just like in a physical inventory, you need to be able to quickly and easily identify and find products or equipment, you need to find information out of your database. Descriptions help greatly with this effort.

There is another reason why field descriptions are useful. When you work with the data in a particular field in *Datasheet* view or *Form* view, you will see the field description on the bottom part of the screen on the left part of the status bar. This is an easy way to help users understand what information goes into a certain field for data entry purposes.

The *Description* is a property that you will find for each main database object. For tables and queries you bring up the *Description* property by taking the following steps:

- Go into the **Design** view for the object
- Click on the **View** menu and click on **Properties**

For fields, the description is part of the table design. For forms and reports, you bring up the *Description* property by taking the following steps:

- Go to the Main Database Window
- **Right click** on the object you want to work with. The shortcut menu will appear
- Click on **Properties**
- The **Description** area will appear

It is important that you enter field descriptions. You want to say enough to distinguish this business item of information from all others in the database. Also, in a field description you can clarify where the information that should go in that field comes from. For example, in a customer database, you may want to keep track of the Duns number. You name the field *DunsNo*. You put in the field description that this is the Dunn and Bradstreet number given for a particular company. You can even mention in the description the location for the Dunn and Bradstreet book in your company or online. Here are some other guidelines you should follow when adding descriptions to your fields in table design:

Always note primary, foreign, and composite key fields. We will discuss these terms and the other new terms mentioned below in the next chapter. If a field fits one of these categories, simply note this in the first part of the description.

If the Primary key field is an *AutoNumber* data type, add the following phrase in your field description: Primary key Field – Number automatically generated by the system.

With foreign key fields, always mention the table and the other field that it links to. You can see this visually in another part of Access, but it helps to write it down. For example, you can write the following description for a *CaseNumber* field in the *Invoice* table: Foreign Key Field: Links to *CaseNumber* field in the *Case* table.

Always clarify which fields will have a pick list for data entry, and where the data source for the pick list comes from. For example, here is the description for the *CaseType* field in the **case** table: Pick list from *ltblCaseType*. Describes what type of case this is from a legal perspective; for example; personal injury, family, or immigration.

Perhaps Miller (2015) says it best when he sums up;

> I have come to the conclusion that no convention is necessarily right or wrong. I have also come to the conclusion that a given standard might be "good" and still not necessarily fit every solution. Ultimately, you need to do what works best for your project, and the conventions I am about to describe may or may not be a good fit for you. If that's the case, then take whatever works and ignore the rest.

Other Considerations

The **Database Administrator** (DBA) is the title for the one who keeps track of these standards and makes sure they are implemented.

The Database Administrator is the person responsible for identifying and taking care of all the data in the organization.

You might say the DBA is a *data accountant* who understands the data and makes sure that it is stored properly, is secured as needed, is re-indexed as needed, is accurate and backed up so that it can be retrieved as needed if the original becomes corrupted. You could say that the DBA oversees the *Fort Knox* for data in that it is valuable and needs to be secure and accounted for. One way to help with this function is to create a "database of the data." This includes at minimum all the table names and field names in those tables, along with descriptions

Chapter Review

We covered how to plan your work by laying out your specifications; starting with the decision to make or buy your database application. You learned a method for defining database requirements and illustrated with examples. You identified time wasters and the importance of scope definition. You also learned guidelines for estimating the time to create a database application. Finally, you learned why and how to use database standards.

Lab

Learn how to create project specification. Create project specification for a personal or an assigned development project. Use the format suggested in this chapter or create one of your own ... OR review specifications for a database someone else is working on.

Apply the Access naming conventions to a database that is already created, such as the *NorthWind* database that comes with Access. You can pull up the Northwind database application by opening Access and then clicking on New. Scroll down to find the Northwind database. When it opens, hold down the **Shift** key before clicking on the Enable message and it will take you to the objects. Pick one table and add a table description. Also pick two or three fields and add descriptions. Pick one query and add a description.

Chapter 3
Set up Tables to Store Your Data

Now you are ready to do the database work. You completed your analysis. You understand the requirements. You have decided on database standards to use. Now comes the most important and probably the most difficult part (conceptually) of database development; setting up the data. Everything else that you do in database development builds on the data. Remember, you are creating a data world that accurately represents the real work world of your organization. You are building the foundation. You must build it firm.

Chapter Overview

In this chapter, you will build on what was discussed in the previous chapter and use the specifications to build your database. You will start by learning how to set up your data in order to meet work requirements. This process of translating the work reality into database objects is called data design. This section will not cover all of the details of data design. However, you will learn the essential principles that you need to meet the design requirements of the real work world. You will learn to set up your fields, create and use indexes, and set up Relationships. You will also see several examples of special data design issues that you will face in your database work and how to resolve these sticky design situations. Finally, you will apply all of these principles by building tables, setting properties, and creating Relationships in Microsoft Access.

Set up Tables to Store Your Data

Goals for Learning

- Understand the importance of setting up your data properly.
- Articulate the Foundational Principles of Data Design.
- Be able to delineate some of the potential problems with table design and how to solve them.
- Learn the two basic approaches to organizing tables and fields (columns).
- Define the different types of keys and the best way to establish a Primary key.
- Learn how to tie together your data with Relationships.
- Understand different join types and when to use them.
- Learn when you need to break table design rules.
- Understand the three reasons why you use data types.
- Learn about the different data types in Access and when to use each one.
- Understand when to set an index.
- Set up your data in Microsoft Access.
- Learn how to find and use data that already exists.
- Learn how to present and agree on your data design.

Questions to Answer as You Read

1. Why do you need to set up your data properly?
2. What are some of the potential problems with table design and how do you solve them?
3. What are the two basic approaches to organizing tables and fields (columns)?
4. What are the three reasons why you use data types?
5. When is it a good idea to set an index?
6. How do you find and use data that already exists?

Terms to Know

Take time to review these terms in the Glossary section at the back of the book:

Attaching
Bottom Up approach to data design
Candidate key
Cascade Delete
Cascade Update
Client-server database
Composite key
Contrived key
Control
Data cleanup
Data design
Data Dictionary
Date type mismatch
Entity Relationship diagram
Field
Foreign key (FK)
Functional Dependency
Importing
Inner-join
Index
Join
Key
Multi-valued Dependency
Natural key
Normalization
Outer Join
Output
Primary key (PK)
Property
Record
Referential Integrity

Relationship
Table
Top Down approach to data design
Transitive Dependency
Validations

Set Up Your Data Properly

Your data forms the foundation of everything else that you do in database development. We emphasized earlier in the book that your data must accurately reflect what takes place in the organization. Now we need to look more closely at how you capture what is going on in the organization with actual tables and fields in a data design. It is important to design your data well for three basic reasons:

1. It allows you to pull out (query) the data that you need to answer questions.
2. It allows you to store information in the most efficient way possible. This allows the computer to pull up the data that you need more quickly (NOTE: although this is somewhat of a moot point these days since computers are becoming more and more powerful).
3. You want the data to be useful. There is a difference between information and data. You might say that gathering information is like playing trivial pursuit. It can be interesting, but not necessarily important. Data reflects the real world in which you work. You want to make sure that you design your tables to capture data that is helpful to you, not just information. If you don't need certain pieces of information, you do not need to capture those pieces.

Let's define **data design**.

> *Data design is the process of deciding which tables you need and which fields you need in those tables to accurately represent the people, things and activities in your real organization and how those people and activities relate to each other.*

Note that **tables** are the building blocks of your data design.

A table represents a particular group, thing or activity in the organization that you want to know about.

We emphasize that it represents a particular group, thing, or activity. A table does not represent more than one item. Remember that you are trying to capture what is really going on in your organization. Tables should reflect this reality. Here are three types of tables and specific examples of each:

- Groups: Employee, Customer, Student
- Things: Matter, Survey, Schedule, Book, Inventory
- Activities: Registration, Work Order

What about **fields**? Fields appear in tables.

A field (also called a column) is a place to store a particular detail that you want to know about a group, thing, or activity (table).

When you set up a table, you want to know more about the item that the table represents. Fields represent those details that you want to know more about. Remember that a field represents a particular detail about the person, thing, or activity in your organization that your table represents. You only want one detail per field.

Many times, people refer to this activity of setting up your data as *database design*. I think that this term is confusing because a database, with most database software products that you will use, includes data but also includes queries, forms, reports and code. I think the term *data design* is more accurate because it refers specifically to that part of the database design where you set up the data in tables.

Deciding where to live is a very big step for anyone. You have to give careful thought as to exactly what kind of house you want to live in. And there is nothing more important to this decision than finding a home with a strong foundation. Yet, this is often the last thing we notice. We are busy looking at the rooms, the closet space; all very important, but the foundation is critical for the house surviving the wind, rain, and wild life that might want to creep in. There are several options for foundations. You can build your home on a foundation of concrete block, caste in plate, reinforced concrete, precast, stores, concrete piers, or a concrete slab. Each type of foundation provides support for the house. You choose a type of foundation depending on the weather your home will face, the wild life situation, the water, and your budget. Your data design will also differ depending on how big a database application you need to build. Some of your databases will face difficult weather in the form of inexperienced users who will tend to enter the wrong information. You need to create a very firm database foundation with plenty of **validations**.

> *Validation means setting up tables and fields and, in some cases, using code in forms to check to make sure that the data entered is correct and disallowing an entry that is not correct.*

Some will design data for a small group of trained database users. A nice concrete (data) slab will do just fine. Even though the foundations of homes can differ, you still need to build them well. This is certainly true of data design.

One final point before we get into the specifics: There is a difference between the data design and the actual **records** (or rows) of data that you store in your database.

> *A record (also called row) is the actual business data entered in a group of fields in a table … like a file folder.*

For example, you can have a table design that includes a table called *Customer* with the following fields: *Company, City, State.* The data stored in the table includes two records (or rows):

Record 1: Cotswold Drilling, Odessa, TX
Record 2: Centipede Tractors, Nashville, TN

Notice that each record is like a row in a spreadsheet; and each record (row) has specific pieces of information that are captured (in this case; company, city, state).

Two Approaches to Data Design

There are two basic approaches to data design. The first approach is called the **Top Down** approach (also called the *Analytic* approach).

> *The Top Down approach to data design involves starting with a basic data design of tables and fields that fits a general business function and then adjusting the design to meet the particular requirements of the customer.*

Use this approach when you are creating an application that is relatively common. For example, if your customer is selling something, you will need tables for *Client* (the people or groups to whom your customer is selling things), *Order*, *Product* (what you are selling with prices and inventory if you are interested), and *Item* (line item within an order). The fields in those tables will differ according to the particular needs of your customer. However, the tables that you need and the basic field structure for those tables will remain similar whether you are selling shoes, lawn mowing services, or books. This is where the table templates in Microsoft Access' Table Wizard can prove somewhat useful. The table templates give you some table structures for doing basic business activities.

The second general approach to data design is called the **Bottom Up approach** (also called the *Synthetic* approach)

> *The Bottom Up approach to data design involves starting with no basic data design of tables, you simply list all the fields that you will need, organize the fields (that represent a similar group, thing, or activity), and then create the tables that you need to contain the fields.*

Use this approach when you are working on a unique project and you may not know how things fit together. You will normally use this approach for the majority of your database projects. In the Bottom Up approach, you may not know how the data will fit together when you begin your data design. But, you do know that you need certain pieces of information. You identify these pieces of information from your analysis work about the organization. You look at the columns on the reports that they currently produce. You look at forms they complete. You remember the questions that they want to answer and the data needed that will give them answers to those questions. You then formulate fields. After designating all of the fields, then you organize similar information into tables. A helpful technique to use here with a group is to put the names of the fields on post-it notes. You can then easily move them around and group them as required. Of course, this can also be done electronically.

Over the last 30 years, different people working in the area of relational databases have identified certain modification problems, classified them, and developed rules for preventing them. When you design a table so that it applies one of these rules, you place the table in a certain normal form. Let's examine the most common kinds of normal form that have been identified and then discuss what all of these rules mean for your database development efforts. The basic acronyms for normal form are the following (name with acronym):

First Normal Form: 1NF
Second Normal Form: 2NF
Third Normal Form: 3NF
Fourth Normal Form: 4NF.

The above items are listed in order of precedence. For example, if a table is in third normal form (3NF), it is also in 1NF and 2NF. Before we look at each normal form in more detail, let's clarify **Functional Dependency**.

A Functional Dependency is a relationship between (usually) two fields where the value of one depends on the other.

For example, if you have pay information and social security information stored about the people in your company, it means that if you know the social security number of a person, you will also know their salary. The salary is functionally dependent on social security number. There is one and only one value for another value.

Finally, a **key** is the field that helps tables fit together.

The key fields establish Relationships in data design.

Foundational Principles of Data Design

Your data design should follow some very basic rules. Eventually, after you have developed expertise, you will follow these rules naturally; or at least break them knowingly. For now, absorb these rules of **normalization**.

Normalization means setting up tables (also called relations) and the fields (attributes) in those tables so that they follow certain rules that prevent errors in the data that you will store. These rules are called "normal form."

Dr. E.F. Codd (1990) developed rules of "normal form" and the relational database model in 1970. His work reflects historical mathematical thinking (set theory). The relational database model states that data is organized in two-dimensional tables (called relations in mathematical terms). Each relation (table) has a number of attributes that describe it. Attributes (mathematical name) are simply fields. So, in this two-dimensional relational model, you have columns (the attributes) and you have rows (the data). Normal form focuses on the rows. You identify potential problems by looking at the data in the rows. However, you fix the problem (or prevent them) by working with the columns. You normally fix the problem by moving certain columns (fields) to new or different tables. As you may surmise, it is best to make these field changes BEFORE you enter any data! But, no worries. Data can be cleaned up to fit in the right place.

As we learned before, your objective as you begin to develop your database is to look at what the client needs to accomplish and to decide which attributes (fields) should be collected together and stored in the same tables. As you create tables, you want to recognize flaws (or problems) in design (also called anomalies) and eliminate them. As we said above, this process of identifying and preventing problems in design is called *normalization*. Each level of normalization is designed to eliminate certain kinds of design problems. The goal of these mathematically-based rules of design is to easily accept additions and deletions in the data without errors. This allows you to correctly answer questions from the data, which is the whole point!

It helps to appreciate the need for rules of proper data design by looking at a few examples of problems (anomalies) that can arise with poorly designed tables. If you have a poor design of your table, you can face problems when you modify your data.

For example, you schedule a student to take a class in Charlotte, North Carolina on November 3. There are also other classes going on in other cities on other dates that other students have signed up for. You name your table *SignUp*. There are four fields (columns) of information that we want to know about the sign-up: *StudentID, Class, ClassDate* and *ClassPlace*.

The data looks like this:

Student sign-up 1: 489, Nov 3, Data design, Charlotte
Student sign-up 2: 621, Nov 10, Excel analysis, Houston
Student sign-up 3: 926, Nov 17, Data design, Columbus

Let's say that student 489 decides not to take the class and you delete that record, you have a problem. Notice that when you delete the row about the student sign up, you also delete information about the date and location of the class. You also have a potential problem when adding data. We cannot enter information about classes until a student signs up. This may not seem to be a severe limitation in this small example but think about it. Suppose you have 10,000 potential students and 63 classes going on in 12 different locations. You cannot easily remember the schedule and to have to keep looking it up to sign up students can be time-consuming, inefficient, and most likely result in inaccuracies. You can solve these two problems by creating four separate tables for *Student, Class* (lookup for *Schedule* table), *Schedule* and *Location* (also a lookup for *Schedule* table). This is the essence of normalizing your data design; identifying potential data entry problems and trying to eliminate them.

Now let's look at the different types of Normal form and review examples.

Normal Form

Data design should follow rules of normalization.

First Normal Form (1NF)

First Normal Form (1NF) just means that you should not enter the exact same information twice in the same table; so, no records (rows) should be exactly the same. It also means that a field should only have one piece of data. So, for example, you would not put *Needham, MA* in the *City* field but should have two fields: *City* and *State*. If you do find that you inherit duplicate data, you need to know how to use queries to clean up your data. We will look at how to clean up data later on.

Second Normal Form (2NF)

A table is in 2NF if it is in 1NF and all of the fields are dependent on the key.

This means that you group things together in a table that really have the same thing in common. For example, suppose you are setting up a training database. You have students who take classes. You do not want to include information about who is teaching a certain class in the *Student* table. The instructor for a class is not related to the student information.

Third Normal Form (3NF)

A table is in 3NF if it is in 2NF and has no **Transitive Dependencies**.

A Transitive Dependency is when the value of a field is determined by a field that is not the Primary key.

For example, suppose you have the following fields in your *SignUp* table:

SignUpID (PK), *ScheduleID*, *ClassName*, *StudentID*, *LastName*.

This table is not in 3NF because the value of *LastName* is not dependent on the *SignUpID* field. *LastName* is dependent on the *StudentID* field. If you change the value of *StudentID*, then the value of the *LastName* field will not be correct. What is the other transitive dependency in the above example? You are right. *ClassName* is dependent on the *ScheduleID* field, not on the *SignUpID* field. As we'll discuss below, your Foreign key field allows you to pull all of the information from the different table when you need it. In the above example, the only fields that you need are:

SignUpID, ScheduleID, StudentID.

If you need more information about the schedule and the student, you can pull up the needed data from the *Schedule* and the *Student* tables.

Fourth Normal Form (4NF)

A table is in 4NF if it is in 3NF and has no **Multi-Valued Dependencies**.

A Multi-Valued Dependency is a situation where for every value of one field, you can have multiple values of a different field.

For example, you have a *StudentCourse* table with three fields: *StudentID*, *Certification*, and *CourseName*. Suppose a student is going for several computer certifications and the courses taken can apply to several certifications. The data appears this way:

43	**Network Engineer**	**Client-Server Architecture**
43	Network Engineer	Network Protocol
43	**Database Administrator**	**Client-Server Architecture**
85	Hardware	Electronics

Notice that the same course applies to two different certifications for the same student, which is a redundancy. To resolve, we should break this table up into several other tables. The key point is that we should replace the *Certification* and the *CourseName* fields with a *CourseID* field. Then we can use the *CourseID* field as a Foreign key field and tie to a *CertificationProgramCourse* table which relates the course to the various certifications to which the course might apply.

Key Fields

Applying relational data design in practice involves an understanding of key fields and Relationships.

Primary key

A **Primary key** field (or key) plays an important role in each table.

A Primary key (PK) is a field (or fields) that uniquely identify each record.

You might say that the Primary key (PK) field *unlocks the door to relationships*! ... because it maintains the integrity of the data (no duplicates) and allows you to relate to other tables for queries. It is very important to identify a good key for a table, because all of the other fields depend on it. You must be careful here to make sure that you pick something that will be unique in all cases. For example, you may have 15 people in your company, so you might decide to use initials as the unique identifier. In this example, initials are a **Natural** (or Federal) **key**.

A Natural key is a field that is used as a Primary key field in a table and represents some characteristic that is present in your organization.

Using initials is fine if your consulting company remains small. However, if the company grows to 350 people, you might have a problem. There is a good chance that you will find people with the same initials. So, when you think of a field to serve as a key, you must look at your situation and how the data will be used.

Sometimes a table will contain a **Composite key field**.

A Composite key field is a combination of two or more fields that together is unique

For example, suppose a student signs up for a scheduled class. One student can sign up for several scheduled classes for a certain semester. So, *StudentID* is not unique and by itself cannot serve as the Primary key field of the Registration table. However, when you combine the student with a scheduled course, you will have a unique identifier. One student will not register more than once for the same scheduled course. These two together; *StudentID* and *ScheduleID* must be unique. You will see this situation in an intersection table (a table used to resolve many-to-many Relationships; discussed later).

In some cases, it is helpful to use a **Contrived key field**.

> *A Contrived key is a field that is created specifically as a unique identifier and does not represent any actual information in the business.*

In a contrived key, the computer normally generates the number. In Access, this is accomplished by using the *AutoNumber* data type. This data type simply gives you a consecutive number as the Primary key field. There are several advantages to using a contrived key field:

1. You can more easily protect the reliability of the data that is entered in the field. When the user has to enter something into the Primary key field, there is a chance that he will not type it properly or might leave the field blank. You can add code to take care of these problems, but it just means more work for you. The *AutoNumber*, makes it very easy to maintain.

2. You do not have to worry about composite key fields. Having two or more fields as the Primary key can prove unwieldy for linking with other tables. You can note the uniqueness of a pair of fields while using your *AutoNumber* field as your Primary key.

3. You can maintain confidentiality. Sometimes a unique identifier may be available, but it may not be appropriate for you to have access to it. For example, social security number is a unique identifier for people but it can violate confidentiality to ask for it. A contrived key eliminates the difficulty of having to ask for this or other potential confidential data.

It is possible for a table to have more than one unique identifier. These fields that are unique identifiers are called **Candidate keys**.

> *A Candidate key is a field or fields in a table that uniquely identifies each record but is not necessarily the Primary key.*

You might say that each of these fields is *running* for the *office* of Primary key. You are the one who chooses which one will serve as the Primary key field. Once you make the choice, you cannot change your mind. Suppose you have two candidates for your Primary key. You have two fields together that are unique, and you also have a field that is an AutoNumber datatype. Both are candidate keys, but the *AutoNumber* field serves as the Primary key.

Foreign Key

A Foreign key field is critical to linking tables together. We will talk more about linking later in the chapter. You want to identify **Foreign key** fields in your table design.

> *A Foreign key (FK) is a field in one table that is a Primary key in a different table and allows you to link tables together in order to share information.*

Basically, a Foreign key field is a Primary key field in a different table and allows you to link with this different table and share data in queries. The link is called a *Relationship*. Let's examine in more detail.

Tying Together Tables with Relationships

Now that we have looked at normal form, let's examine some general guidelines for how to build tables. As we mentioned in our previous section, as a database developer you want to do all that you can to prevent errors in working with data. Any good database development software (like Microsoft Access) will allow you to build in protection for your data. This is done by laying out your tables properly and establishing **Relationships**.

> *A Relationship is a link that you make between tables based on a common field that allows you to use data from both tables in your outputs.*

The first thing that you want to examine is how fields relate with each other. You might think of a database as *a spreadsheet that can relate well.* You establish a Relationship between tables by **join**ing a common field (or fields). Notice that Database Design involves not only creating things (people and activities) that appear in the organization, but also determining how they relate with each other so you don't have to duplicate data.

> *A join is the act of actually connecting two common fields together from two different tables. This is the means by which the Relationship takes place.*

The Join (or link) will be either a one-to-one Relationship or a one-to-many Relationship. Once you establish the link, your database software can apply rules (also called *triggers*) to make sure that your related data remains accurate. There are three logical ways that tables can relate with each other.

One-to-One Relationship

In this situation, for every data value in one field, there is only one similar data value in a different field. For every *StudentID*, there is one *LastName* that goes with the *StudentID*. For example, if there is a record in the *Student* table where the *StudentID* = 28828, then there is only one record in the *TrainingPlan* table where the *StudentID* = 28828. You will place fields with a one-to-one Relationship in different tables. In this situation, for every record in one table, you can have at most one record in another table. There are three situations when you may need a one-to-one Relationship between two tables.

First of all, for security reasons, you do not want other people to see certain fields in your table. For example, you might have an *Employee* table with all of the employee information (which many people can see) and a separate table called *Salary* with just the confidential pay information for each employee (which only a few can see). *EmployeeID* is the Primary key field for both tables and for every record in the *Employee* table, there is only one record in the *Salary* table.

Secondly, there might be certain fields that do not apply to everyone else. For example, if an employee has a spouse, you want to keep certain information about the spouse. However, suppose approximately 35% of your employees are single. For these people, all of the spouse information will be null. Normally, you want to set up your data so that there are not many nulls in a certain field for many of the records. If there are many nulls in a certain field, you should eliminate the field because you don't need it or move the field to a different table. By moving the spouse fields to a separate table called *Spouse*, you eliminate unnecessary nulls in the *Employee* table. Again, *EmployeeID* will be the Primary key field for both tables.

Thirdly, you might not have control over certain data, so you create a separate table with the custom fields that you want. Then link it to the table over which you have no control. There are situations in organizations when someone else controls a table but the table does not contain all of the fields that you need. You don't want to tamper with the table set up by someone else. You can solve the problem (in Access) by linking to the table and then creating a second table with the additional fields that you require. You then set up a one-to-one Relationship with the other table.

One-to-Many Relationship

If one actual data value has many possible occurrences in another table, this is a one-to-many Relationship. For example, in a business each *Individual* has only one mentor. However, each mentor can have several individuals assigned. In this situation, you only include one field from the *Mentor* table in the *Individual* table, the Primary key (*MentorID*) field.

Many-to-Many Relationship

If one actual data value has many occurrences in one table and possibly many occurrences in another table, then you have a many-to-many Relationship. For example, in a business situation, each individual can take many different classes. Also, a scheduled class can have many different individuals attending. You cannot depict this type of Relationship by working with two tables. You have to create a third table (sometimes called an *intersection* table) composed of at least the Primary keys from the other two table. You can have additional fields in this third table as needed, but you must at least have the Primary keys from the other two tables. So, to show a many-to-many Relationship between an individual and scheduled classes, you create a third table called *SignUp*. This table indicates which individuals sign up to attend which classes.

Using Relationships to Protect Data Integrity

Let's continue our discussion about protecting the data by talking about **Referential Integrity**.

> *Referential Integrity means that when you have a Relationship between two tables, you are linking the proper record(s) together; each and every record in one table matches the proper record in the other table.*

This also means that each record in the child table has a parent record to refer to. Each record in the child table has a Foreign key field with a value that refers to a record (matching Primary key field value) that actually exists. Of course, the reverse is also true; that when you do not have Referential Integrity, your actual data is not accurate because a Relationship is broken. By looking at an example of how Referential Integrity is violated, we can get a better idea of why it is important. Two tables are joined; the *Class* table and the *Schedule* table. *ClassID* is the Primary key in the *Class* table and *ClassID* is the Foreign key field in the *Schedule* table; providing a link to the *Class* table. Now suppose you have actual data that looks like this:

The *Class* table contains fields *ClassID* and *ClassName*

HIST450	**Modern European History**
HIST500	Ancient Civilizations

The *Schedule* table contains fields *ScheduleID*, *ClassID*, *Term* and *Classroom*:

101	**HIST450**	**Fall, 2018**	**EVANS 122**
103	HIST500	Fall, 2018	EVANS 318
104	**HIST450**	**Fall, 2018**	**FANUEL 34**
108	**HIST450**	**Spring, 2019**	**FANUEL 34**

We have scheduled the Modern European History class (HIST450) three different times. You run a report that shows all of the upcoming classes. Now suppose you change the value of the *ClassID* field in the *Class* table for the Modern European History class from HIST450 to HIST550.

What happens when you run the report for upcoming classes? You will not see any classes listed for Modern European History. Why is this? Well, because you changed the value of the Primary key field (in *Class* table), the Foreign key (in *Schedule* table) no longer matches. You have a problem! The records in the *Schedule* table that contain HIST450 in the *ClassID* field no longer have a reference. Referential Integrity is violated. Each record in the *Schedule* table needs to refer to a record in the *Class* table.

Let's look at another example. Suppose you have a student who takes many classes (in the *SignUp* table). One of the fields in the *SignUp* table is the *StudentID* field. The *StudentID* field serves as a Foreign key field in the *SignUp* table and allows you to link the two tables and share data in queries. Now suppose a student (Student ID is 57) drops out who has taken four classes. You delete the student (57) from the *Student* table. Now you have a problem. You have four records in the *SignUp* table with a Student ID of 57, but these records have no place to relate. They are orphans in that they have no place to go.

You solve this problem by making sure that your data design enforces Referential Integrity. When you enforce referential integrity, it means that your database software (in our case Microsoft Access) will not allow you to delete a record or change a Primary key field value in the main table when there are records in the linked table with the same field value as a Foreign key. Notice that you are creating a rule that prevents people from deleting or changing (Primary key field value) a parent record when there are children in another table for that parent record. If you want to delete the parent record, you have to first delete each child record.

Once you enforce Referential Integrity, you also have the option to use **Cascade Update** or **Cascade Delete**.

Cascade Update means that when Referential Integrity is enforced, if the value of the Primary key is changed in the main table, all of the values of the Foreign key fields in the linked table will be updated with that same value.

Cascade Delete means that when Referential Integrity is enforced, if a record is deleted in the main table, all of the records in the linked table with the same key value will also be deleted.

In the preceding example, when you delete student 57 from the *Student* table, the four child records in the *SignUp* table are automatically deleted. This is a Cascade delete. Deleting the parent record causes a cascade down to the child table so that the other records are deleted. This is good because you maintain Referential Integrity. The obvious problem is that you lose valuable data that you might want to use to produce reports. If you do choose to use Cascade delete, you normally archive the details before deleting. We will discuss archiving later in the book.

Cascade update works in a similar manner. In our previous example, when you change the value of the *ClassID* field in the *Class* table (for the Modern European History class) from HIST450 to HIST550, the related records in the *Schedule* table are automatically changed. The value of the *ClassID* field in the *Schedule* table (Foreign key field) will automatically change to HIST550. Keep in mind that it is NOT a good idea to change the value of your Primary key field. But if a user does this, Referential Integrity insures that the data will remain consistent.

Setting up Joins

When you join two tables, you can determine which part of the data between the two tables to display. This feature of data design emerges from mathematics and Set theory. Let's explore the two basic types of joins and when you will want to use them:

1. Inner-join (this is by far the most common type), also called *Equi-join*
2. Outer-join (used to include all of the data in one of the tables).

The **Inner-join** is the default type of join in database applications (including Access).

An Inner-join is a type of join where the only records that are included from either table are the ones that have a common field value.

Another term for describing this effect is that you are finding the *intersection* between the two tables. Notice your situation. You cannot have a sign-up unless you have a student. The data from the *SignUp* table is contained in the *Student* table. So, you use an inner join (again, the default) when you are interested in seeing a report of students who are taking classes.

However, it is possible to have students who are not signed up for classes. You may want to see a report of the courses status of all the students, including the ones who have not taken classes yet. This will allow you to follow up with those students. Use an **Outer-join** for this type of situation. An Outer join shows the *union* between two tables.

> *An Outer-join is a type of join where all the records from one table are included and the records from the other table that have a common field value with the first table are also included.*

As mentioned above, an Outer-join is needed if we want to include the records from the *Student* table whether or not there is a matching value in the *SignUp* table. Suppose you have 20 students and you want to show information about the courses they have signed up for and taken. You will use the *Student* table and the *SignUp* table. Now only 17 students have signed up for and taken a class. If you created a query with the two tables and created the usual Inner-join, you would show only 17 students and the details of their classes on the output. Change the join in the query to a Left Outer-join and then you will see the other 3 students listed with no details from the *SignUp* table.

You should not set up Outer joins when you create your Relationships in Data Design. This will cause confusion and possibly cause you to lose flexibility. When you want a particular kind of output (query result and/ or report) that requires an Outer join, set up the Outer join in your Query Design.

When you are building a database application from scratch, you should define Relationships and establish Referential Integrity on those Relationships. If you are working with data already present in your organization, you may not be able to set up Referential Integrity because the data is bad. Sometimes it can help to create an **Entity Relationship Diagram**.

An Entity-Relationship Diagram shows the items in the organization, how they relate to one another, and perhaps how this activity in the organization translates into data design.

When and How to Set Indexes

Use **indexes** to increase search performance.

An index is a special file stored in the database that increases performance.

When you choose the field that will be the Primary key (in Table Design view, click on field and then click Key option from menu). Notice in the properties for that field, that an index is indicated with "No duplicates." This makes sure that each record is unique.

An index is like the back of the book. Suppose you want to read about the Hittite empire in Asia Minor in a book on ancient civilizations. You could flip through every page and visually scan for the word *Hittite*. A better way is to go to the back of the book and look for the word *Hittite*. You find that the Hittites are discussed on (for example) pages 43-58 and page 183. Boom! You quickly move right to the proper pages. This is how a database index works. Now a computer can "flip through pages" very quickly, so consider setting an index (one of the field properties).

The rules for when to set an index:

- You will search or sort on this field.
- There are a wide range of entries in this field.

Suppose you have a field called *Region* with only four regions in a table with 8,000 records. Indexing does not help. Again, in our book example, suppose 25% of the book is about the Hittites. If you simply flip through the pages, there is a good chance that you will find out something about the Hittites. So, there is really no need for an index to find this information.

You do not have to index on a field to sort on that field. Remember, the index just makes your search faster in certain situations.

Stretching the Rules

Now that you understand some important principles, let's look at several situations when you may want to violate these rules. As Al Foster put it (1990): "Those who use databases and eat sausage would probably be more comfortable if they didn't watch either being made. But if efficiency, clarity, consistency, and quality are the goal – and they are – then end users not only have to watch, they have to help stuff the sausage." (p. 42)

Unstable Data

One of the difficulties you will find when working in the database arena is bad data. Another issue is accessibility. You may not be able to obtain the data you want when you want it. Another factor is performance. You may only want to work with a sub set of data instead of all of the data. For example, you have a central database listing people in the company. However, you do not have control over this database. You want to build a database for your local work group that references this data, but you cannot count on the fact that the data will remain consistent enough to keep a Relationship. For example, people are signing up for training classes and you want to keep track of what takes place. There is a chance that one person could sign up for many training classes. The challenge is that you want to keep track of information about the person but it is possible that the information can change for that individual. So, you may just want to download people information and save it in your local database to make sure that the data will be there when you need it (given that security is in place and there are no legal issues!).

Impact of Reporting Requirements

A variation of this situation exists when you want to keep track of the totals for a given department (i.e. for charge back purposes). Individuals can move between departments. If a data design is truly relational, you will have a table for the people in the organization and then you will reference that table when you sign up the individual for a class. But there is a potential problem. Suppose Rebecca Wilson signs up for *Personal Time Management* while serving in the *Accounting* department. Two months later, she moves to the *Marketing* group. She then takes the class on *Leading an Effective Meeting*

101. Now, when you calculate the total classes taken for each department for the quarter, you have a problem if you keep a purely relational design for your tables. In a relational design, when Rebecca changed departments, you simply change her department field in the *Personnel* table. Now when the quarter ends, both classes will be credited to the *Marketing* group. In this case, you have to include the department field in the sign-up table and pull in the current department data when the person signs up for the class. You could keep a separate change table, but this is more unwieldy. Let's look at some other particular issues when you might want to violate the rules of normal form.

Names

It is often difficult to take care of all of your reporting needs by simply using the last name and first name of an individual. Issues arise such as; what name do you use for the first name? Do you use the full first name, like *Joseph*, or do you use the first name that the person prefers to be called, like *Joe*? You might want to use full first name and first initial for the address on an envelope and a different option for the salutation on a letter; such as title and last name. It all depends on what people prefer and your output purposes for the data. Things are further complicated when you have families involved. Are you interested in sending something to the entire family or to one of the members of the family? This will decide how you structure your data. Finally, what if you want to use the name in a legal document? The full name in all capitals is required. There are techniques in Microsoft Access for forcing text to all capitals, but it might be more convenient to capture the full name in all capitals in a field called, for example, *LegalName*. However, it is ONLY in this rare case (and really even this case it is not required) should you use all capitals when storing data. Otherwise, always store your data in lower case (or title case).

Because of the need for flexibility in using names, you sometimes have to stretch the rules of normal form by creating more than one field to contain name information. Also, you might have to combine entities in the same field to meet all of your requirements. So, you might want to include some or all of the following fields in a table for keeping track of people:

Title: Title of Individual (primary point of contact). Pick list of options including: Mr., Mrs., Ms., Miss, Dr., Rev.

LastName: Last Name of Individual (or family)

FirstName: Full First Name of Individual (of primary point of contact for the family

Salutation: Name to include on salutation in letters. (Includes spouse if married)

Envelope: Full name to include on name line of envelope or return address in a letter. (Includes spouse if married)

FirstNameCalled: First name by which person wants to be called (primary point of contact)

Spouse: Full First Name of spouse

SpouseCalled: First name by which spouse wants to be called.

Keep in mind that this list is meant to give ideas; it is not meant to be determinative. Again, you have to decide what data needs the table has to meet. For tracking families, you usually want to create two tables; one for the family information (*Family*) and a second table for the individual information (*Individual*). In the *Family* table, include the *LastName, Envelope*, and *Salutation* fields. In the *Individual* table, you will want to consider including the same fields (*LastName, Envelope*, and *Salutation*) along with the *FirstName* information. Why do we include *LastName* in the *Individual* table? It is because it is possible for a family member to have a different last name through a second marriage, choice, or other circumstance. Your data needs to be flexible enough to handle different people's preferences. If you are using the data to keep track of people, it is important to communicate with people in a way that they prefer. People's names are meaningful and your data design should reflect that importance.

What about the situation where you have a list (like a donor list) and you have individuals and companies who need to go into the same table? One solution is to add a field called *Company* to the table. Here is where you can enter the company name if it is a company. You can use the name fields to enter the information about the point of contact in the company. You can also include a field in your table called *Type*. Make it a Number data type (Byte). The entries for this field will be *1* if it is a family and *2* if it is a company (you can set up an option group on your form). You can then create *IIF* statements on your queries to show different fields on your reports depending on whether the record is a family or company. In a sense you are combining different entities in this situation (because they have slightly different characteristics), but it is often more manageable to do it this way.

Notice how these suggestions actually violate our rules for normal form. However, they give you the flexibility that you may want to meet your organizational needs.

Addresses

Closely related to names, is how to deal with addresses. Address information also requires some special considerations. How many addresses do you need, not to mention phone numbers? Also, what about the street addresses? For companies, do you need separate addresses for mailing and for the physical location? Do you need two or more fields for the street address; especially when entering the information for a company?

Obviously, you want separate fields for *Address*, *City*, *State*, and *Zip*. But do you really need a second address field called *Address2*? This would violate some of the rules by having the same entity in the same table, but sometimes it is useful; if, for example, you want to include Suite number or the name of a building in the address line. It is possible in Microsoft Access to place the second line of an address in the same field. However, again, this breaks data design rules. Generally, you use one address line for individuals and two address lines for companies. For individuals, you normally do not need to store both the home and the work addresses.

Another challenge is when you have several addresses for the same entry; like in an ordering system where you have an address for credit card information and an alternate address (or addresses) for shipping. Technically, you should create a separate table of addresses if you have more than one address for the same person. However, many times it is smoother to just create a second set of addresses in the same table for shipping or as an alternate. You can also add a field to indicate which address is the active address for certain actions; like mailings, for visiting, or for legal items.

The same problem applies to phone numbers. You may want to create a separate table for phone numbers (called *PhoneNumber*) with three fields (four if you want to add an AutoNumber Primary key): Foreign key to link the *Individual* table, the phone number, and a category field (Pick List) which delineates what kind of phone number it is (Home, Work, Cell, Other). However, most data designs are served well by adding three phone number fields in the table with the name and address information: *PhoneWork, PhoneHome, PhoneOther*. The alternate phone can be a cell phone or other work phone. Again, you might include a field which indicates the phone number that is best to use. So, when phone lists are generated that call for one phone number, you can use the one that is most useful. You should consider adding a memo field to a table on individuals called *Comment*. If you have to store additional phone number or addresses, you can put them here.

Regarding the entry of phone numbers, it is recommended that you not use any data entry mask (one of the properties available when you set up your fields). Just make your phone number fields text data type without any mask. This gives you much more flexibility in the way you enter phone numbers. You can easily include international phone numbers and extensions if you do not include the mask.

Tracking Activities

Here is another data design conundrum. You want to track activities of an individual or an event. For example, you want to create a Personal Development Plan for individuals in your company. Normally, you will create a second table (to relate to the *Person* table) called *PersonalDeveopment* which includes fields such as: The Primary key from the *Person* table as a Foreign key, the Primary key from the *Activity* table (which contains a list of different development activities that are available) as a Foreign key, and maybe a *DateDue* field and a *DateCompleted* field. You build the Personal Development Plan by assigning activities and due dates to an individual in the *PersonalDeveopment* table. Then you track the progress of the person by entering the date when the activity was completed. This situation is fairly straightforward.

However, what if you are tracking recruitment? You might have a different situation. Maybe EVERYONE goes through the same activities when it comes to recruitment. They have to mail in a resume. You want to note that you sent them a letter of interest in reply. They mail in the completed application. You conduct an interview and maybe have a rating or comments about the interview. So, you can see that it is possible, since all the activities are the same for everyone, that you could simply put these fields in the *Person* table. You can do this by simply adding check box fields for the different tasks that need to be completed and perhaps dates when completed.

Once again, this goes against the grain of proper data design. You can imagine one of the pitfalls; suppose the list of what is required changes? Then you have to redo your table design or assign new attributes to a field instead of changing data in a different table. However, in many cases the check list approach can get you up and running quickly and is a good way to keep track of when actions have been taken on an individual. You can also see where it is very easy to determine which individuals have completed activities and which have not; which is basically what you want to know if you are following up people.

You are almost ready to get into the nuts and bolts of creating a data design in Microsoft Access. But before we do, let's talk more specifically about how to go about setting up the data that you need. We will do this by talking about fields; which are the building blocks of tables.

What to Include in Your Tables

Now that you know what data design is and why it is important, let us look at more of the particular activities you need to add to your repertoire to continue growing as an excellent database developer or leader of database development. In this section, we will discuss exactly how to figure out what fields to include in your tables. Note that this activity may well overlap what was covered in the previous chapter. In other words, you have to think of the data design so that you have the information needed to create an accurate proposal.

Understanding what to include in your tables is the most exciting part of database work; and the most frustrating. You have the opportunity to create a data design that is excellent and really meets the need of your customer; or you can create a data design that is a flop and will totter and fall at the slightest demand for information that actually helps productivity. Do not worry, you will not flop. You will succeed. You can do it. One of the most important ideas that you need to keep in mind when you start designing data is that data design is an art. Every situation is different. Remember, you want the data design to reflect the actual work situation. To reach this goal, you have to be creative. However, within that creativity, there are very special rules that you need to follow. You might say that as an excellent data designer, you are a top-notch freestyle ice skater. If you have ever watched an ice skating event, you know how creative the routines are; coordinating music, hand gestures, costume; with varied skating movements, twirls, and jumps. The effect is breath-taking. But, the ice skater uses very specific skating techniques as the foundation for the entire routine. These techniques stay basically the same. New ones are added occasionally. The techniques are used in different combinations; maybe with different arm movements, different variations of a common technique. But, the foundation remains. This must be true in data design. You must understand the principles that we will cover in the rest of this chapter, but you will only gain true understanding of data design rules by actually creating a database yourself.

The key to understanding the fields that you need to include in your tables is looking at the **output** that you want to produce in your organization.

> *To output your data means to show certain pieces of the data in a certain format on the computer screen or on a piece of paper from the printer. The output shows you answers to questions from the data.*

Take time to look at the different reports that you currently produce (which you should obtain as you carry out meetings to plan your work). Make sure that you look at daily reports and summary reports that you want to produce for a certain time frame. When considering reports, make sure that you have people be very specific as to what they want. Insist that your users show you a copy of what they currently produce or sketch out on a paper exactly how they want the report to look. This will help you flush out your data design and will also give you a head start in preparing the reports you need for your application. Make a note of output that is already stored electronically. This is important because the electronic media may contain data that you can bring into your tables. This will save you much time in having to reenter the data. We will talk more about this topic later. The rule of thumb is that you strive to NEVER reenter data that already appears in an electronic format but clean up the data first and then import (sometimes the order is reversed, import and then do the **data clean-up**); the main thing is that you clean it up!

> *Data clean-up involves making sure data is in normal form (mainly removing duplicate data) before using. This is accomplished by using queries.*

You can determine what data is needed by examining what people produce and by talking to people. Look at forms that people fill out, how they are stored, and how the data is used. You want to avoid capturing meaningless information. Always strive to capture data that will help improve your organization, without violating people's personal privacy. You can also talk to key leaders in the organization as well as workers (the ones who fill out forms and run reports).

Data design is difficult because it is very Aristotelian; because you have to figure out what is repetitive and what isn't. You have to be tenacious about the details. Most people don't like this. It goes against the flow of current culture. But remember why you use a database; because a database is specially created to store information efficiently and retrieve it in a very flexible manner. You will be different because you will do the tenacious work necessary to capture critical information in your data design.

On a final note for this section; note how data design overlaps with our previous section on specifications. In some sense, you have to carry out the data design to create the proposal. Each situation might be different.

Understanding and Using Data Types

Setting data types is one of the steps that makes a database function as a database and not something else. For example, you can store data in Microsoft Word or Microsoft Excel; but not efficiently. And it can prove difficult to retrieve your data. Setting the data type, however, allows a database to work much more efficiently with the data. Keep in mind, however, that things are changing: for example, data used in analytics can have no data type. However, we could argue that at some point, it is brought into a database format for analysis purposes.

Data types help in several ways. Historically, this has increased performance by allowing more efficient storage (less hard disk space) and quicker retrieval; however, not as critical now. Data types guard data entry by making sure that you put the right kind of data in the right place. For example, if you go to a field that is a *number* data type, and type "Hello Bill" and press the **Tab** key, you will receive an error message. Finally, data types impact how calculations are carried out. For example, if something is a *date* data type, Access knows that 11/18/2017 – 10/18/2017 = 30 days.

The bottom line is that you use data types because you HAVE to! But at least the above explanations help you better understand why. When you are working with your data, particularly writing queries, it is important that the data matches the data type of the field with which you are working. Otherwise you will run into a problem called a **data type mismatch**.

> *A Date type mismatch is an error (usually in a query or when entering data) that occurs when the data that you want to work with is a different data type than the data type that the field requires.*

Now let's look at the particular data types in Microsoft Access and when to use each one. Each DBMS will have slightly different choices for data types. However, they all are very similar. So, reviewing the data types of Microsoft Access will equip you to work with data types for other database products.

The basic rule for setting data types is this: make the data type as small as possible while still handling the largest potential data entry in that field. Let's briefly examine the Access data types and when to use which one.

Text

This is the most widely used data type, because you can type anything in a Text field including text, numbers, and punctuation. You can enter up to 255 characters per record in this type of field. You are constrained by the size of the FieldSize **property** that you set when you design the table.

> *A property is some characteristic that you can change about an object.*

To allow a maximum width of 255 for a field that is a (Short) Text data type, you change the FieldSize property to 255. Fortunately, Microsoft Access is flexible regarding the way it stores Text data. It only stores the size of the value actually entered into a field. For example, suppose you have a field *LastName* that is a Text data type with the FieldSize property set to the value of 50. You enter a last name *Atkins*. Access only stores the 6 characters from that name, not the 6 characters plus 44 blank spaces.

Remember the second part of our rule for data types; you have to handle the largest possible piece of data that will be entered into that field when you set up your data type. If your field width for a Text data type is not wide enough, you have a problem. Access will not allow you to continue typing and you will not be able to enter the rest of the information. Suppose you set up a Text field called *Description* and you make the field width 50. You begin typing in a course description that is rather lengthy. All of a sudden, you cannot type any additional text. If you want to enter the additional characters, you need to increase the FieldSize property of the *Description* FieldSize property.

Of course, you use the Text data type for entering text information and combinations of text and numbers. But you also use it for entering other types of information such as zip codes, phone numbers, and apartment numbers. The rule is that if you are not using the field in calculations, make it a Text data type. For example, you are not calculating phone numbers so you should make phone number fields Text. This makes sense when you think about it. Suppose you have a zip code that is 02194. Normally, a Number data type will not display the first zero but will automatically remove it. You can use the Format property to get around this, but still there is a problem. What if you happen to have the last 4 digits of someone's zip code and you want to add a dash and the last four digits: like this: 02194-2311? With a number data type, you cannot do it. With the Text data type, it is not a problem. It is recommended that you make your FieldSize wide enough to handle variations with this kind of data; especially phone numbers. You should give yourself a FieldSize of around 20. This will allow you to handle international numbers, business extensions and any other constraints that are needed.

One idiosyncrasy of Text fields is how it sorts data. This is not a problem when you are only working with text data but it becomes a problem when you are working with data that combines text and numbers. For example, a code like ZZ230 is sorted before ZZ31 because the first number that Access sees (the 2) is less than the 3. Notice that it doesn't take the number 230 as a whole, but only digit by digit.

If you have to have a certain sort order with text and number data, the best way to handle it is to add a field to the table called *SortOrder*. You can make this field a Number data type and then enter the proper order in here. This can be tedious, but it will always give you the proper order.

Memo (or Long Text)

The Memo data type (can also be called *Long Text*) is like a Text data type except that you can enter more information. You are not limited by the 255 characters of the Text data type but can enter basically unlimited information. This gives you a tremendous amount of flexibility in data storage. Of course, the disadvantage of the Memo data type is that it does take up more storage space than the Text data type. Also, you cannot create an Index (we will talk about this shortly) on a Memo field or sort by a Memo field. However, you can search a Memo field to find information contained anywhere in the memo field. This is very powerful feature of Access.

There are several situations when you might want to use the Memo data type. It is good to include for things like comments, descriptions, and logs. If you are taking care of customers and want to detail a conversation with a particular customer, you can enter the gist of the conversation in a *Comment* memo field. If you have a catalog of equipment and you want to enter detailed descriptions, you can create a *Description* Memo field. Finally, if you are following up on the purchase of a piece of property, you can maintain a log of all of the actions taken on that purchase by date by creating a *Log* memo field. The only thing to watch for in these situations is whether or not you want to total the number of interactions or otherwise put a number as part of the entry and then want to calculate them. The Memo data type will not allow calculations of data entered. If you do want to calculate the data in some way for all of the records, you would want to create a separate table of comments or log items and link it to the main table.

Number

Use the Number data type to handle any numbers that you want to store and use in calculations. The Number data type is very powerful and useful, but it is critical that you understand the FieldSize property of the Number data type. The best way to think of the FieldSize property for numbers is that it practically gives you basically six different number data types with which to work. Here are the six different FieldSize options for the Access Number data type (NOTE: you will also find these options in other databases; but with slightly different names and in other databases these options will sometimes appear as separate data types).

Byte: Equal to or Less than 255; decimals not allowed; 1 byte of storage required.

Integer: -32,768 to 32,768; decimals not allowed; 2 bytes of storage required.

Long Integer: -2,147,483,648 to 2,147,483,647; decimals not allowed; 4 bytes of storage required.

Single: After 10 places to left of decimal, stores exponentially. After 7 places to left of decimal, rounds rest of numbers to 7th digit; 7 decimals allowed; 4 bytes of storage required.

Double: After 12 places to left of decimal, stores exponentially. Does not round rest of numbers after 7 places to left of decimal; 15 decimals allowed; 8 bytes of storage required.

Decimal: Flexible. You determine the number size allowed in the field by setting the Precision property for this field; Decimal places are flexible. You determine the number of decimal places allowed in the field by setting the Scale property for this field; 12 bytes of storage required.

So, you can see that you have several options when using the Number data type. You have to give some thought as to what is required for your data. Again, the rule of thumb for picking a data type applies when choosing a Number data type; pick the smallest FieldSize that will still handle your largest possible entry. It is helpful to look at the list above and determine what criteria you will use when determining the FieldSize of your Number data type. What categories do you see in the list that will help you evaluate your need? If you look carefully, you will find three criteria:

1. Size of number that you will need,
2. The number of decimal places,
3. The storage space taken up.

When you choose the Number data type, Access defaults to the Long Integer (or Double) field size. Notice that the Long Integer field size takes up 4 times more storage space than the Byte field size. This is not a big problem in smaller databases but can affect performance in larger databases. So, give some thought as to what types of numbers you need the field to store. Again, it is better to err on the side of having too large a field size. If you try to enter a number that is larger than the field size (or contains decimals if your field size is Byte, Integer or Long Integer) then you will receive a Data type mismatch error message.

As stated before, you use the Number data type to store numbers that you often use to perform calculations. There is another use for the Number data type. An Option Group is a particular kind of control that you can use on a form. If you plan to include an Option Group in your form, you want the corresponding field to be a Number data type with a field size of Byte.

There are two other numeric data types in Microsoft Access. These two are more straight-forward to set up than the Number data type. They do not have the confusing FieldSize property options to worry about. Let's look at the Currency and AutoNumber data types.

Currency

Always use the Currency data type when working with money. The type of currency is determined by your operating system settings. The reason you need to use the Currency data type is so that the rounding of your financial calculations will remain consistent with financial practices.

AutoNumber

The AutoNumber data type is a special kind of number that adds the next number each time you start adding a new record. Keep in mind that the number in the AutoNumber data type is incremented at this point whether or not you save the new record you are creating. The AutoNumber field starts with the number *1*. This field always increments to the next number. When records are deleted in the table, the numbers are lost and will not be replaced. There are two ways to reset the AutoNumber counter to *1*:

1. Delete all the records in the table and then Compact your database (under **Database Tools**, or **Tools** and then **Database Utilities**) and then choose **Compact and Repair Database**.

2. Make a copy of the current table by using **Save As**.... and then Append the data from the original table but do not append any field value into the AutoNumber field of the new table. This action will reorder the AutoNumber data type consecutively.

The AutoNumber data type will prove valuable to you as a Primary key field; establishing such things as Part Numbers, Student IDs, Course Number. The AutoNumber data type is actually a Number data type with a FieldSize of Long Integer. When you use an AutoNumber field as a Foreign key field, you always change it to Long Integer.

Remaining Data Types

Date/Time is another data type. Again, you can change the display of your date by changing the properties. Always use this data type with dates and time items so you can calculate properly. Use the Yes/No data type for marking list inclusion (if there are no other distinguishing criteria), like noting that a sales lead wants to receive email updates. You would also use Yes/No for marking completion. The field type is also called *Boolean* or *Logical*.

The OLE Object data type allows you to store pictures, files and other objects in your database. You have the option of storing the item directly in your database, which takes up storage or linking to the file location. If you have a stable system for storing your object files, I recommend using the link option. The Hyperlink data type is somewhat similar but you only link to the Web.

Setting Properties

As mentioned, always update the Description property for each field. Update other field properties as needed. Let's look at a few other properties available in Microsoft Access Table Design view that you want to keep in mind.

Format: As mentioned, set for Number data type.

Label: Use this property. What you put there will be what the user sees on a form or even in Datasheet view. This is another way to make sure the user knows what data this field represents. See, table design is more involved than you thought. Look how you will save yourself time in the long run. Once you define a label, every time you use that field in a form or report, the label will faithfully appear.

Validation: Use this and the Validation Message properties to enter a business rule for entry. Just be careful because users will not be able to enter anything if the rule is violated and they may not know why so make sure the Validation Message is clear if you use the Validation property.

Required: I recommend not using. Only key fields normally require an entry and that will be automatically done without using this.

Default: OK if, for example, you default to a certain state for addresses.

How to Find and Use Data That Already Exists

If there is data somewhere in the organization that you need, find it and bring it into your database as needed so that you can use it. You do not want to have to re-enter data and you want to avoid having data in several different places.

You find data that already exists by doing "data detective work." In other words, as you gather specifications, you also find data that already exists and catalogue it. Then you build a **Data Dictionary**.

> *A Data Dictionary is a "database of the data" and includes all organizational databases and all tables and fields included in those databases.*

When you are just getting started, data may be in all kinds of places in the organization (i.e. Excel and Word lists). You want to find them and put them in database format and record in the data dictionary. You also need to understand the data structure of any ERP database that you are using so that you can attach and use with other data as needed. Normally the ERP will have its own Data Dictionary so may want to keep separate or combine with yours. The DBA is the person charged with setting up the data dictionary and "watching over" the database; which includes, installing, backing up, restoring if needed, and securing (among other things).

Now you are ready to use that data by **importing** or attaching.

Importing means to bring outside data into your database so that there are two copies, the original and the copy that is now in your database.

Importing is relatively straightforward. Normally, you would want to import data into a separate table and then clean it up before adding to a table in the database. Normally you would import lookup lists or other static data. You would also import data from other formats. The main thing to remember is that if you import data into your database, you should maintain that data in the database and not in the original source. In fact, it might be a good idea to delete the original sources so that users won't be tempted to keep using the old files. The rule for you as a data management leader is always keep data that keeps changing in one place.

Attaching is a second way to use outside data.

Attaching means to use outside data with your database so that there is only one copy, the original.

Normally, you will not change any attached data but are just "borrowing" it to use in queries and reports. Keep in mind that (given you have permissions to do so), any changes you make on attached data will be changed at the source. So, if you are attaching tables from your ERP, it is probably best to make them "read only."

Make sure you have installed the Microsoft Open Database Connectivity

(ODBC) driver so that you can attach to **Client-server databases**, like Microsoft SQL Server or Oracle.

> *A client-server database is a larger DBMS that puts the data on a server (locally or "in the cloud"), called the "server" or "back-end," and puts everything else in a separate place, usually on the user machine, called the "client" or "front-end."*

Your ability to access any client-server databases will be controlled by the DBA for that database, so you would need access and login credentials to attach.

How to Present and Agree on Your Design

It is not enough to create a good design. You must make sure that two other things take place: you must make sure that your design truly reflects what is important to the business. Also, you must make sure that your decision maker(s) agrees to this design and signs off on it. Printing out a picture (i.e. Entity-Relationship Diagram) of the overall design and the details will help you achieve your purpose. Printing out your design can help you understand your layout and can help you communicate the structure to others. This also can prove very helpful after you have finished your project to give users guidance on the names of fields so that they can run queries.

In Microsoft Access, you can create and print out your design by going into **Database Tools** and clicking on the **Relationships** button. Line everything up and then choose **File** and **Print**. You can also export in *html* format. Put this in your system documentation.

You can also print out the details of the table design so that you can see the descriptions and more details about the fields. Do this by clicking on **Database Tools** and then clicking on **Database Documenter.** This will get you started on your Data Dictionary.

Now it is important to obtain agreement on the design. Make sure you work with your development team that you set up originally. You may already have approval if they signed off on your proposal. Make sure all the data fits properly. Make sure you can answer the business questions that the organization needs to answer.

Once set up, DO NOT change field names. This is bad. Keep in mind that you will refer to these fields in all of the rest of the parts of your database application: in queries, forms, reports, and code. The only time you could change a field name is if there is NOTHING else in the database and no documentation has been printed. Other than this one, isolated situation, you will create major problems for yourself if you change field names. Keep in mind that if you have to, you can change the Caption property for the field or the form Label property for the control so this should suffice.

Chapter Review

We learned how to set up data in order to meet work requirements. We also looked at rules of data design and how to adjust to accommodate unique design situations. We covered the specifics of data design; including setting up fields, creating indexes, and establishing Relationships. Finally, we covered how to apply data design principles by building tables, setting properties, and creating joins in Microsoft Access.

Lab

See if you can design the tables for a Training Management System. Create a new database. Link to the *Employee* table in the *NorthWind* sample database. Then create the additional tables needed, including identifying keys. Don't forget to also add descriptions and appropriate indexes.

Chapter 4
Create Queries and Reports to Answer Questions

Chapter Overview

Chapter 4 covers queries and reports; applying the database standards that were discussed previously. The emphasis of this chapter is on using queries and reports to answer questions. But, we will also discuss the important use of Action queries to help implement business processes; as well as gathering data for reporting purposes. Advanced query development techniques are also discussed to enable you to develop complex, flexible queries.

Goals for Learning

- Understand the power and flexibility of database queries.
- Learn how to create and execute queries.
- Learn how to select appropriate data sources.
- Create calculated fields using other database fields.
- Enter query record selection criteria.
- Understand Action queries and their uses.
- Learn how to archive data using queries.
- Understand how to use queries to implement business processes.
- Understand how to use queries for decision support.
- Realize that SQL is the building block for queries.
- Create reports.
- Understand the Report Design environment.
- Understand how to combine queries and reports.

Questions to Answer as You Read

1. What is a query?
2. How do you design a query?
3. What is the difference between a Select query and an Action query?
4. What is the role of queries and MIS?
5. How do you use queries for data maintenance activities?
6. What standards should be applied to query names?

Terms to Know

Take time to review these terms in the Glossary section at the back of the book:

Action query
Archiving
Bound control
Calculated fields
Data sources
Dynaset
Expression
Expression Builder
Function
Parameters
Query
Query Design Grid
Record selection
Sections (in reports)
Select query
SQL
Unbound control
Wizard

Foundational Principles of Query Design

A **query** is a question or request for action.

A query is a question asked about data contained in the database tables or action that needs to be taken. Queries are created and can be stored as database objects.

"What is your name?" is a query. Database queries are questions asked about the data contained in the database (which, again, reflects what is really going on in your organization). "Which projects have unbilled hours assigned to them?" is a database query. You might say, it's like playing the old TV game show *Jeopardy*, where you start with the answer and then figure out what question to ask to get the answer. The query is the question that provides the data answer that you want.

Database queries can also be defined as a request for action such as "List all projects with unbilled hours assigned to them." Both approaches will return the same results. The questions which will be asked and the actions required by business activities need to be defined in your specifications. Once the database tables have been defined, then queries are developed to answer the questions or perform the required actions in your database application.

Queries may use a single data source or multiple data sources. Tables and other queries may all be query **data sources**.

Data sources are the tables and fields (from those tables) used as input to a query.

Each query creates a unique **dynaset** each time the query is executed.

Temporary virtual tables created by execution of a query. A new dynaset is created for each execution of a query and only includes records and fields selected in that particular query. Dynasets are available for use by other database objects.

If two users invoke the same query, two dynasets will be created, one for each query. Query dynasets are database objects accessible by other database objects such as forms, reports, and other queries. The dynaset is the answer to the business question. The dynaset contains only the fields defined for the query and only contains the records selected by the query.

Care must be exercised when viewing the results of Select queries in either Datasheet view or using forms. As mentioned above, Select query dynasets are linked in real-time to the underlying tables. Modifications to data or record deletions made in a Select query dynaset are immediately made to the data in the underling table. This real-time link between query dynasets and tables enables powerful queries to automate business processes and database maintenance processes.

Two Types of Queries

There are two major categories of queries; Select queries and Action queries. A **Select query** simply retrieves the requested data.

> *A Select query simply retrieves the requested data in the format and order requested and displays it.*

Note that Select queries (along with, for example, Crosstab queries) can be included as one of the subcategories under *Show* queries (not covered in this book) because they display the data versus acting on the data. Select queries extract and display selected data from tables or query dynasets. Select query results are presented in a column and row format similar to an Excel spreadsheet. Select queries display a restricted amount of data from one or more tables or other queries, based on the selection criteria used in the query.

Select query dynasets can be used as input to Action queries, forms, and reports. Select queries with multiple data sources are used to combine data from several tables or query dynasets.

An **Action query** performs specified actions on database tables.

> *An Action query makes changes to the requested data and does not display it.*

Action queries are useful for such things as; helping implement business processes, data clean-up, **archiving**, and importing.

Archiving is the process of extracting and storing historical business data which is no longer required for current activity but maintained for decision support and analytics.

In most cases, you should always run a Select query first to make sure you will be impacting the data you have in mind. Once the results of the query have been confirmed, you can change the query to the appropriate Action query and execute the data changes. ALWAYS (except perhaps when rollback is in place for a particular transaction entry) back up your data before running Action queries. If anything goes wrong, you want to be able to restore your data!

Calculated Fields

Calculated fields are often used to calculate values based on data contained in other fields in a table.

Calculated fields are fields created in queries which do not appear in any database table. They are used to display data calculated from other table fields and, like a regular field, can accept record selection criteria.

Calculated fields can also be called *non-database fields* because they are not fields in the table design; since they must be recalculated each time they are displayed. For example, a Select query might display employee age. Each time the query is run, ages must be recalculated based on today's date and the employee birth date. Let's assume that *BirthDate* is a field in the Employee table. The calculated field in the query would look like this (Note that we give the calculated field a Label called *Age*, which shows in the resulting dynaset):

Age: DateDiff("yyyy",[BirthDate],Now())

You can see that it might be helpful to create a program (which we could call *CalcAge*) that could perform this calculation anytime that it was needed. We will discuss programming later in the book. (Note that in the above example, we would also need to add an IIf function to evaluate whether or not today's month and day was greater than or equal to the *BirthDate* month and day. If not, then need to subtract 1 from the total. If so the above **expression** would work).

> *An expression is a combination of values, operators, functions and object identifiers which are put together to find a result you are looking for.*

Similarly, a Select query might display the days remaining for uncompleted projects based on today's date. Given that we have a field called *CompletionDate* in the *Project* table, the expression might look like this:

DaysToCompletion: DateDiff("d",Now(),[CompletionDate])

Another Calculated field might show total sales by using fields from the, for example, *OrderDetail* table. Assume *Quantity* and *UnitPrice* are fields:

Total:[Quantity]*[UnitPrice]

Calculated fields are used in queries, forms and reports to provide the required data without necessitating complex procedural updates of time sensitive data. Select queries may have complex **record selection** criteria, including using Calculated fields.

> *Record selection is the process of including or excluding records from a query dynaset. Record selection criteria are user defined.*

Summary Queries

Summary queries give totals from the data, usually on a category. For example, you may want to pull the total sales by product from the *Product*, *Order* and *OrderDetail* tables. So, your query would include the *ProductName*, and a sum on the *Total* Calculated field (as described above). You could also add *OrderDate* (would not show it in query results but only for criteria) and pull sales for a certain time frame. You could then use this dynaset to create a bar chart which would easily show which product sold the most. If you have a large number of products, you could use *ProductCategory* to generate the totals. As you can see, Summary queries are powerful tools for analysis.

Crosstab Queries

Crosstab queries are a special type of Summary query. Crosstab queries summarize the values of selected records and fields into user-defined groups or total levels. Crosstab queries perform arithmetic functions such as count, sum, or average on selected fields. Crosstab queries present their results in a column and row format similar to an Excel spreadsheet. Crosstab query dynasets contain only the summarized data and not the detail records used to accumulate the summaries. Normally, the only way to get details and totals in one place is in a report.

Input for Crosstab queries may come from other tables or query dynasets. A query displaying the total hours by project for each customer is an example of a Crosstab query. Note that the difference between a crosstab query and a summary query is that the crosstab query adds a dimension. In the above example, a summary could only show total hours by project but would not break it down by customer. This would be fine if there was only one project per customer. But it could not show a total if there were several projects per customer. The Crosstab query allows this another dimension; each customer. Crosstab queries are a powerful tool for providing Management Information and Decision Support reports and data.

Action Queries

Action query examples include:

- Append: Append queries add records to existing tables.
- Delete: Delete queries delete records from the target table.
- Make-Table: Make-Table queries create new tables from records and fields in the dynaset.
- Update: Update queries modify the values of selected fields in existing tables.

Append Queries

Append queries add records to exiting tables. Records in the Append query dynaset are added to the target table. Records in the Append query dynaset must meet all the data integrity requirements of the target table.

Append queries are often used to create archive or historical data table entries; followed up by a Delete query to remove the archived data from the live system. Append queries are a useful tool in maintaining Decision Support tables. Append queries are also a valuable development tool especially in data conversion.

Delete Queries

Delete queries delete records from the existing target table. Input for Delete queries may be from other tables or query dynasets. Delete queries enhance the integrity of the database by automating the deletion process based on records selection criteria. This eliminates deleting the wrong record by accident. Select queries showing record counts are often used as input to delete queries to visually verify the amount of data to be deleted. Records deleted by Delete queries cannot be recovered. Again, this is why you should back up your data before running Delete queries.

Make-Table Queries

Make-Table queries create new tables from records and fields in a dynaset. Make-Table queries are an invaluable development and conversion tool. Select query dynasets are almost always the input source for Make-Table queries. Make-Table queries may combine fields from multiple records into a new table. Often multiple Select query dynasets are combined to create a new, unique table and record format. All existing field properties of each field in the dynaset will be carried forward to the new table. There is no permanent link between query input tables and the new target tables which are established. When trying to build complex queries, it is sometimes easier to make (temporary) tables from dynasets and then use them in new queries to get the data you need.

It is important to distinguish between the Append query and the Make-Table query. The Append query adds to an existing table and the appended records must match the data types of the fields in the existing table. The Make-Table query creates a new table whose structure is defined by the record format of the Make-Table query dynaset.

Update Queries

Update queries replace the values of selected fields in existing tables with different values based on criteria. As always, run a Select query first to insure data integrity, and then run the Update query. Update queries significantly enhance the quality of and accuracy of data in the database. Utilizing Update queries to apply hours to projects or payments to customer balances are examples of enhancing data accuracy and quality. Human math or posting errors are eliminated by successfully implementing Update queries. Update queries are valuable tools in automating business processes (Management Information System).

Applying Queries to Business Processes

The technical skills to create queries are easier to master than the analytical and design skills required to effectively apply the correct query type to the appropriate process. It is often necessary to combine multiple query types to provide an effective solution to a particular business problem or to automate a business process. This section presents the application of queries to a variety of business processes. You will apply the query selection criteria just discussed to practical business process examples. It is not possible to list all potential situations you will encounter; but these examples will give you a good start.

Queries and Transaction Processing Systems

Transaction processing systems support the daily activities of business operations. Transaction processing for something like a consulting database would include creating and maintaining customer and project records, entering time to be billed to each project, preparing and sending invoices to customers and collecting money from customers. Other examples might include making a reservation or placing an order. Forms would be used to enter the data. Since forms can be restricted to specific fields, there is little advantage to using a query with a data entry form.

Since both forms and reports will operate on tables, you are probably wondering how queries apply to transaction processing. We will use the process of entering your billable time and updating project and customer records as an example. After entering the time for each project, you will need to update the hours for each project and the billing records for each customer. Update queries can automate both processes. You could create one Update query to apply those billing hours to both the project and customer tables. Creating an Update query for each table will provide additional flexibility in the automation of the billing process. The design specifications developed in creating your proposal will determine whether you will use one or two queries for updating billable hours. The decision of one or two queries should be based on user preference unless there is a compelling design requirement dictating one option. For example, assume your proposal specifies that customer records will not be updated until an invoice has been created. The billable time entered into a billable time table via a form would be input into a number of Action queries. Each Action query would automate a portion of the billing process.

The business process of billing project time involves several steps. Each of these steps must be accomplished in sequence. Each billable time entry must be matched to the appropriate project and customer records.

1. Update the hours billed to each project
2. Create invoices for customers
3. Update each customer's balances.

Updates to the project and customer records may be done manually. However, that process leaves the data vulnerable to error. You might post to the wrong project or customer. You could make a math error in recalculating balances. You might enter an incorrect number into a record. It is your responsibility as a business leader overseeing your databases to look to provide automated processes which help insure the accuracy and integrity of the data. Developing queries to automate the updating functions of the billing process will provide greater assurances of data validity and integrity.

Now let's look at how queries can automate the functions in the billing process and increase the accuracy and integrity of the data.

1. The billable time table would be an input for an Action query which updates the hours in the project table. The hours in the billable time

table would be added to the total hours for each project. This same query or another Action query would flag each billable time record to indicate the project table had been updated. Query logic would prevent records flagged as updated from being processed multiple times. Both of these Action queries would be Update queries.

2. Records flagged as having updated the project table would be input into another Action query which would create invoices for each customer. Billable time records used to create invoices would be added to an invoice table and flagged as having been processed to create invoices. Again, query processing logic would prevent duplicate processing of records. An Append query would add new records to the invoice table. An Update query would flag the records in the billable time table as having been processed for invoicing.

3. The customer table balances would be updated using the billable time records which have been flagged for invoice processing. It would be possible to update the customer table when the invoice table records are created. It is a better database design approach to keep each query limited to one major purpose. Using simple queries designed for a single purpose also provides greater flexibility in maintaining the database over time. Also, keep in mind that you can use a macro or code to run several queries all at once.

4. The last Action query helps manage the billable time table records. Records which have been flagged for project update and invoice processing will be archived into a processed billable records table using an Append query. Archived records can then be removed from the billable time table using a Delete query.

Also use Action queries to archive and then delete activities. Both queries will be developed with the same selection criteria to insure they select the same records for archiving and deletion. The alternative would be to visually inspect each record to determine if it should be archived or deleted. Using queries to automate these activities avoids human error and thus enhances the integrity of your database.

It is important to note that the sequence of these Action queries determines their effectiveness in automating the processes.

1. The project Update query is the first in sequence.
2. Followed by the invoice processing queries.
3. The customer table balance Update query is the next in sequence.
4. The archive and deletion queries are the last queries in the sequence.

Another set of Action queries needs to be developed to post payments received from customers. Payments received from customers are entered into a payments table using a form.

1. The payments table is input into an Update Action query to maintain the balances in the customer table. These payments are flagged as having been applied to prevent reapplying the same payment. Which balance fields are updated is determined by your design blueprint.
2. Another Update query modifies the project table to accumulate payments received for each project. This step will be required only if your blueprint design specifies a need to track payments by project. If the project table is updated, only records previously applied to the customer balances should be used. This would insure that customer credit has been applied before accumulating payments for each project. Which process occurs first, customer payments or project payments, is a user design issue. The sequence preferred by the users will dictate the sequence in payment processing.
3. Finally, payments which have been applied must be archived and purged or deleted from the payments table. An Append query and a delete query accomplish these table management functions.

Again, the sequence in which these queries are implemented insures their effectiveness in automating the payment posting process. All required Update queries must be accomplished prior to the Append query. The Delete query will be last in the sequence.

Let's recap what you have learned about transaction processing queries. Your systems design proposal defines both the business transaction processes and the queries which will support them. Automating these business processes provides a higher degree of assurance that the systems will maintain both data validity and data integrity. Action queries permit the automation of business transaction processing. Action queries should be limited to one major action in the process. Query sequence is critical to their effectiveness in automating business processes. Maintenance and archiving of transaction records are vital parts of the transaction processing business function. You should plan for these functions in your blueprint.

Queries and Management Information Systems

Management information systems provide information for the control and evaluation of the transaction processing function activities. Reporting is the primary function of management information systems. Select queries dominate the database activity for this function. The deletion and archiving activities discussed in transaction processing are sometimes included as a management information function, but our focus will be on reporting and inquiry activities. The details of building reports and forms are developed in later chapters. This section deals with the relationships of queries to forms and reports; and deploying them to provide the required management information reports and form inquiries. Again, the development of selection criteria will be covered later in this chapter. The emphasis here is on developing appropriate and flexible queries for input into reports and forms.

Reports and form inquiries may operate directly on tables. However, using queries as input to reports and form inquires greatly enhances the power and flexibility of these database objects. Multiple table queries may be developed as input to reports and forms. The ability to easily combine fields from multiple tables significantly expands the power of reports and forms. Developing queries for input for reports and form inquires also provides increased functionality and flexibility for the database. Databases are normally designed for multiple users. Even your consulting database should be designed for multiple users as your database consulting business grows.

Just how do queries enhance multiple user databases? Remember that queries create a dynamic dynaset each time the query is executed. Reports and forms then operate on the query dynaset instead of the actual tables.

This leaves the tables free to accept new data, perform table maintenance functions, and provide the same records for other queries, forms, and reports. Creating queries for input to reports and inquiry forms enables concurrent table access by multiple users without requiring complex database administration techniques. More people can access more data with less database management effort.

We will continue our example of the business processes supporting billing customers for time spent on each project and collecting funds and tracking payments. This section will not address the detailed specifics of each report and form. Again, the development of record selection criteria will be presented later in this chapter. Our focus here is on designing queries and combinations of queries that provide the data for complex informative reports and inquiry forms.

Form inquiries allow users to review a record or group of related records. Using forms enhances the look of the user interface of your system and provides extremely flexible options to present data. The development of forms will be presented in later chapters. Transaction processing forms will normally operate directly on tables to capture and validate data quickly. Inquiry forms provide quick and easy access to data about a specific customer or project. Let's consider the following scenario as an example.

A customer calls asking about the number of hours they have been billed. Now you must locate that customer's data to answer their question. You can search through the customer table or locate a printed report and search for their data on the report. But, a faster and better alternative is to use an inquiry form to quickly locate the required data. You simply open the form, enter the customer identification code and their data appears in the form. There may be several forms and subforms linked together to provide further billing detail about the customer.

1. A Select query is created with an input parameter that accepts the customer identification code from a form to retrieve the appropriate data.
2. An inquiry form is created using the query created above as input.
3. Control buttons are added to the form to enable inquiry into the billing data detail for the customer.

4. Queries are created to show the billing detail for each of the customer's projects. These project queries select project billing records using the customer identification code of the original query as a selection criterion.

5. Subforms or other linked forms are created to show the billing detail for each of the customer's projects.

These queries and forms provide instant access to the same customer billing data that may be present on billing reports. Form inquiries offer significant advantages over printed reports. First, they are always current and easily accessible. Secondly, forms and subforms can be linked to provide increased levels of detail as you navigate through the form set. All data in the form set pertains only to the customer in the original form and query. You might have to look on multiple reports to provide the same level of detail contained in one form set. Finally, using forms and queries expands user access to data. Several users could use the same form set to answer questions from a number of customers. Providing that same level of access for multiple users would require each user have copies of the reports. Forms and queries increase user efficiency and reduce operational costs.

It is important to remember that all types of queries are available for you to develop complex reports and form inquiries. Select and Crosstab queries will provide the final input to reports and forms. However, multiple Make-Table, Append, and Update queries may be combined prior to the final Select query. You should fully explore the power of using these combined query combinations as processing activities to build extremely complex reports and form sets.

Queries and Decision Support Systems

Decision support systems provide analytical information supporting strategic decisions. *What if?* analysis is an important part of decision support. Decision support systems do not monitor or control transaction processing activities. However, decision support systems utilize transaction processing data when performing analysis. Normally, the goal is to gather data that you can export to a spreadsheet for *What if?* analysis. You then can analyze what has occurred to determine what could occur or what would happen if you changed some variables such as price per hour for specific types of projects. Decision support often requires recalculation of current transaction processing data. Since you cannot change transaction processing data for your analysis, a temporary analytical set of data must be created. A Make-Table query can be used to create new tables from selected subsets of transaction processing data. Decision support analysis will not use all the fields or all the records of the transaction processing tables. You may even need to combine fields from several tables into one analysis table. Decision analysis also often requires several iterations of variable changes against the same base data.

Developing queries to create analytical tables enables you to easily and quickly produce multiple sets of the same analytical data for comparison of variable changes. Show queries are used to provide flexible analysis and presentation of decision support data. For example, a Crosstab query enables you to quickly and accurately summarize data on several fields across multiple tables. Make-Table queries using multiple tables as input can quickly produce analytical tables. Append queries can quickly add additional data to existing analytical tables. Update queries provide a flexible method to apply several iterations of variable changes to the same data.

Using queries to create and update decision support analytical tables has two major benefits.

1. First, it protects transaction processing data from inadvertent corruption.
2. Second, it provides a consistent and accurate method of creating and updating analytical data.

This makes the analytical process easily reproducible and reusable in the future. The effective application of queries enables you to provide flexible manageable decision support data while maintain the integrity of transaction processing data.

Similar techniques are used for analytics but, as mentioned earlier, the main difference is that analytics uses very large sets of data (*big data*) and, as stated in the definition, uses external data and data in non-traditional formats (like clicks on a Web page).

Queries as Development Tools

Queries can be invaluable tools in the development process, particularly in the testing and validation phases. Queries developed to support development and testing processes will not be used by your customer. They are for your use in developing, testing, and implementing the database system. This section will provide examples of how you can utilize queries as a testing and development tool. During development you will need to convert data from any existing electronic form to your database structure. You will need to test and validate all automated processes. Queries provide the means to accomplish both. Test and development queries must be readily identifiable so that they can be removed from the production database that you deliver to your customer. Naming of test and development queries is covered below. You will have at least two databases for each system you develop or work on. One will be the customer's production database they use to conduct business. The other database also belongs to your customer but is used exclusively for system development and testing. The system development database contains testing and development queries, the production database does not.

Queries as Conversion Tools

Data exists for all software application systems. Sometimes, the data may not be in electronic form, but it still exists. Part of your tasks as a database developer is to convert the existing data into the correct format for inclusion into the new system (as we discussed previously, also called data clean-up). Data that is not currently in an electronic format must be entered into the new system. Data that is in an electronic format should be converted or transformed into the new format. Conversion is preferable to simply entering the data into the new system. Entering the data into the new systems creates too many opportunities for human error causing data inaccuracies and inconsistencies. Converting the data from the current electronic form to the new format eliminates the potential errors of entering the data. Queries provide an efficient means to convert data.

Data conversion requires the data to be in some electronic format. You should import the data first and then you can use in Access queries. Other electronic formats such as delimited text files or electronic spreadsheet files should not be used as sources for queries. There are two simple conversion rules you should strictly adhere to. First, you should always retain the original data format within the development database for the new system. Second, you should also maintain converted data at the completion of each stage of conversion. Both rules may be easily adhered to using queries. The original data format from the old system is imported into a table. There should be at least one table for each source from the old system. For example, there should be one table for employees, another for customers, another for vendors, etc. Retaining these tables in the development database insures you will always have the original data that was converted to the new system. There are often multiple stages to data conversions. Creating conversion queries and conversion tables enables you to follow the second rule. This insures that the conversion process is well documented and reproducible if necessary.

This section will not detail the planning or execution of data conversion. We will explore converting data formats as examples of using queries in the conversion process. These examples assume you have the current data in an electronic format and follow the same basic steps.

1. Import the old data format into a database table.
2. Create tables which define the new data formats.
3. Use Action queries to transform or convert data from the old to new format.
4. Set Text FieldSize property.

Text field lengths of the old and new system may be different. An Update query may be used to move data from the old field length to the new field length. The old data format is the input source and the new format table is the update target table.

As mentioned in the Data Design section, numeric data formats may be different. The old system may have more or less decimals in the numeric format. The new format may be currency while the old format was not. Again, an Update query is used to convert the data format with the original format as the source and the new format as the update target table. One word of caution in converting numeric data formats; it is better to use a compute statement rather than simply moving the data from one field to the other. The compute statement better insures proper format conversion.

Queries as Testing Tools

You must test all aspects of the system you develop. Every form, every report, every query, and every automated process must be tested. Developing queries can assist in the test and validation process. Queries created for testing and process validation will not be a part of the production database system but will remain in the development database. You should explicitly identify test and validation queries to readily identify them and allow you to remove them from the production database. Naming test and validation queries is discussed in the next section. Most of your test and development queries will be Select queries which you will use to validate the business processes you have automated. We will continue the example of automating the billing process to illustrate applying queries to the test and validation process.

There were four major steps in the automated billing process.

1. Updating project table hours and flagging records in the billable time table that had been processed using Update queries. Select queries can be developed which will total the number of hours and records flagged in this automated process. You could also create queries showing total hours for each project. Running a project totals query before running the Update queries provides base comparison numbers. Running a project totals query after the update provides new totals which should be equal to the pre-update totals plus the update hours. A query on the totals of flagged records validates the flagging process.

2. Creating an invoice record for time billed to each customer and flagging billable time records as having been invoiced using Append and Update queries. Totals for each customer should then equal the customer totals for the invoices created in this process. Select queries provide those comparison totals.

3. Updating customer balances for hours billed using an Update query and flagging billable time records used in this process. Select queries

to the customer update and record flagging would parallel the test Select queries for the project table update. Both customer totals update and record flagging could be validated using Select queries.

4. Maintaining the billable time table by archiving billable time records which had been processed in the previous three using an Append query. Archived records would then be deleted from the current billable time table using a Delete query. Show queries will provide both record counts and totals for comparison of both the archive and deletion processes. This verification process insures your record selection criteria are accurate.

These totals validations could be done manually, just as could the updates of each of the tables. Using queries automates the validation process.

Building Queries

This section will present you with an overview of Access query building tools and techniques including; query source selection, record selection criteria, and other techniques. Developing an understanding of these tools and techniques will enable you to apply them throughout your database development career to whatever challenging situations you may encounter.

Now let's look at how to set up your queries. This includes determining fields, sort order, and creating Calculated fields; as well as setting criteria.

Query Tools

Access has two query building environments, the Query **Wizard** and the Query Design Grid.

A Wizard is a development tool provided by Access tool for quickly creating query, form and report objects. Modifications cannot be made using the wizard.

The Query Wizard quickly builds simple Select queries from a single source. This section will not discuss the Query Wizard. If you are reading this book, you should avoid the Query Wizard and always go directly to the **Query Design Grid**, also called the *Query Design View*. Query Design provides a robust development environment enabling you to develop any type of query and selection criteria the situation dictates.

The Query Design Grid is a fully featured query development tool in Microsoft Access that allows you to create queries using multiple tables and/or other queries and provides the ability to set criteria and query type.

The following sections detail using the Query Design Grid for source selection, query type selection, record selection, and query enhancements. Just keep in mind that as you continue to develop your database skills, that you should eventually move to learning and being able to use **SQL** to build your queries.

SQL (Structured Query Language) is the accepted standard for writing queries. Syntax may vary slightly depending on the DBMS you use.

For example, when you create a query in Query Design, Access actually translates into SQL for processing.

You access the Grid in Access by clicking on **Create** and then clicking on **Query Design**. As you can see, you first select the tables you need for your query. If you have linked the tables in your data design, they will automatically link in the Query Design Grid. Otherwise, you can create the link in the Grid by clicking and dragging the Key fields. Now, add the fields that you want to the Grid. Then add any criteria you would like (discussed later).

Source Selection

The Query Design Grid affords access to all data source database objects, both tables and queries. Any combination of tables and queries may be selected as input sources to a new query. This flexibility provides unlimited access to all database data source objects. The Query Design Grid also recognizes the Relationships you may have established between tables. The end result of choosing tables with established Relationships is a

Join between those tables. Joins relate data records between multiple tables. Proper selection of source objects, records, and fields enhances the power of queries. You control the content of the query dynaset through source, record, and field selection.

A query may have several tables as input. Table A is related to Table B and Table C is related to Table B. A query may select data fields from all threes tables and relate them into a new record set in a Select query. The results of this query may never be displayed but only serve as input to, for example, a Make Table query which creates a temporary, or perhaps permanent, table containing the combined data; which you can then use for a report or export to Excel for decision support analysis.

When should you use tables for query input and when should you use query dynasets as query inputs? There is no direct answer to that question. Your decision on query input will be determined by the purpose of the query and the output required from the query. What inputs are required? What outputs are required? Are the outcomes temporary or do they need to be maintained for a period of time? Your design proposal will determine which sources are required for each query. Your options for combining tables and query dynasets as input sources or comparison value sources are unlimited.

Query Type Selection

The Query Design Grid allows the creation of any type of Select query or any type of Action query. You need only to select the appropriate types of query using the Query drop down menu on the Menu Bar. The design grid changes for every type of query providing different requirements and options for each. This section will not detail the specific steps for building each query. You should become familiar with the design grid for each query type. The Query Design Grid also provides the capability of creating queries in SQL. There is no requirement for any SQL knowledge to use the Query Design Grid. However, database developers with a working knowledge of SQL may create queries using SQL rather than the Query Design Grid.

Record Selection Criteria

Recall the previous section of this chapter where you applied queries to the specific business process of billing time and recording customer payments. Step 2 in the billing process selects only those billable time records flagged as having updated the hours fields in the project table to create customer invoices. Likewise, in step 3, records flagged as used to create customer invoices are selected to update balances in the customer table. The record selection sequence follows the updating, archiving, and deletion process sequences for the billable time table.

Record selection can be made from either the design grid or from the Expression Builder tool. The **Expression Builder** is invoked by selecting the Magic Wand icon on the Query Design Toolbar.

The Expression Builder is an Access Tool for building criteria for query record selection and query processing.

Queries provide complex record selection, regardless of the method used for developing the selection criteria. Comparison operators enable testing of specific field values for record selection. Comparison operators include equal, greater than, less than, and not equal. Logical operators enable complex record selection on multiple criteria. Logical operators include And, Or, and Not. The full list of Comparison and Logical operators can be found in the Expression Builder tool.

The window in Expression Builder is divided into two halves. The top half is where your selection criteria are captured. Control buttons appear at the side of the data capture area and operator selection buttons appear below the data capture area. Selection criteria may be typed directly into the data capture area of this half. However, simply using Expression Builder to manually enter selection criteria does not take full advantage of this powerful tool.

The power of Expression Builder lies in the bottom half of the window which is divided into three sections. The far-left section lists all the available database objects. You may select any object by simply clicking on the object name. This section resembles Windows Explorer in organization. The types of objects appear as folders which contain all defined objects of that type.

Folders for in-built functions, constants, operators, and common expressions also appear in this section. The center section lists the contents of the object selected in the left section. The field names appear in the center section as an object is selected. The functions folder lists all available types of functions in the center window. The same is true for constants, operators, and common expressions. The right section displays declared values for fields in database objects and syntax for common expressions. The right section also displays the functions, operators, or constants of each type selected in the center section.

A detailed discussion of all the contents and options of Expression Builder are beyond the scope of this book. You should explore Expression Builder and experiment with its options and capabilities to develop your own expertise in using this powerful tool. A sound functional understanding of Expression Builder can save countless hours in the development process. One extremely important advantage of using Expression Builder is correct syntax. Expression Builder generates correct syntax for all functions, operators, expressions, and constants. More importantly, Expression Builder generates correct syntax for database object names. Selecting database objects in Expression Builder insures that there will be no syntax errors in naming the objects. Correct syntax coupled with the flexibility and sophistication of Expression Builder will prove invaluable. As you experiment with Expression Builder you will come to appreciate it more and more.

Record selection capabilities may be further expanded by using the *If-Then* logic commonly found in program code. Access fully supports *If-Then* logic in either the Query Design Grid or in Expression Builder. Expression Builder is recommended for developing *If-Then* logic. Remember that Expression Builder generates correct syntax for database object names. Creating *If-Then* logic in Expression Builder frees you from the sometimes-tedious task of correcting the syntax for database object names and allows you to concentrate on the *If-Then* logic. Complex *If-Then* logic with multiple, nested *If-Then* statements allow you to create powerful and flexible record section criteria.

Flexibility and Sophistication

The Query Design Grid and Expression Builder permit the creation of Calculated fields in queries. These objects are called expressions and may be defined in any query. Expressions are similar to Unbound controls (discussed later in book) used for Calculated fields in forms and reports. Query expressions become a part of the query dynaset and are fully accessible by other database objects. Expressions may be used within the query in record selection criteria, even *If-Then* logic. Creating query expressions is much like creating internal variable data elements in program code. Expressions can be used to create input **parameters** for queries.

> *A parameter is a value that gives input to a function. The value is entered or pulled from another object when the function is run.*

Remember the example of a customer Select query which requires the entry of a customer identification code. The entry of the customer identification code returns only the data for that customer. Without the input parameter, you would have to step through each record until you located the correct customer. Access has the capability to create expressions and use them as variables within queries and between queries and other database objects. Expressions greatly enhance the power and flexibility of queries and enable you to apply your creativity to develop extremely sophisticated query sets.

Creating Reports to Use Your Information

Reports may be considered printed queries with additional capabilities. Reports are questions asked of the database which are presented in a printed (or electronic, like .pdf) format. Reports serve several purposes. You might design a report detailing all activity on each project or all activity for all customers. The invoices created in the transaction processing discussion earlier are reports. Customer statements are also reports. The Access report generator is a powerful tool allowing input from multiple sources on the same report. Using queries as input sources significantly increases the power of the report generator, especially in complex reports with multiple sources. Remember that queries build dynasets, and once the dynaset is created, the table records are released. Complex reports from multiple table sources can be an inefficient utilization of the database. Building the same reports from multiple queries increases the efficient utilization of the tables without decreasing the efficiency of the reporting operation.

When to Create Reports

Reports are like finally sitting down and enjoying a wonderful meal. You have planned the meal. You have asked everyone what they like. You have bought all the ingredients. You have followed the directions and cooked everything to perfection. You have set the table. Now you and everyone else can enjoy the fruits of all your labor. The meal tastes delicious. It satisfies. You thoroughly enjoy masticating every delicious morsel.

Reports are the fruition of all the other work you have done. This is where you experience the real power and versatility of a database. If you have planned well, creating reports is a satisfying experience. If not, it can very disappointing as you realize you need information that you have not stored.

Having said this about reports, in many cases, simply running a query can give you the information you need to answer your business question. So, let's go over when and how you might want to create a report.

Like queries, you might want to generate certain reports depending on the business need. For example, an invoice would be a transactional report. As part of an order transaction, you would set up the system to generate an invoice in a .pdf file format so that the customer can download or can be included in an email or printed and mailed (the envelope would be generated as well). For a training operation, you might need to generate an official transcript that will print on special paper.

You might want to generate a report to support management information that gives operational status regarding, for example, sales goals versus actuals. These can be run on a regular basis to give managers needed information for operational decision-making. Again, you can set up your database application to automatically generate these reports and even send. Or, as mentioned above, you can display on the screen.

Decision support reports are a bit different. In many cases, you will be creating a query or report table (created from a Make-Table query) that can be loaded into Excel for review or graphing. You can also then set up to run *What-If?* analyses for help with decision making. Other tools, like Tableau, can also help.

The techniques you use to create reports in Microsoft Access are very similar to other report generator tools from other DBMSs. You start with a data source for the report, normally a query created specifically for the report. You then use the different sections of Report Design to place text, fields and graphics to show details and totals needed.

Before we get into the specifics, we need to understand the difference between Bound and Unbound controls.

Basically, a **Bound** control will show values from a field.

> *A Bound control is a control on a form or report that shows data from a field*

An **Unbound control** does not show a field value.

> *An Unbound control is a control that does not show data but can show calculations or other information like text*

You should know a bit about the Report Design environment first before using the Report Wizard. Otherwise, you may not understand the available options in the Wizard.

The Wizard is not necessarily a bad option when quickly creating reports. As always, first create and save the query you want to base your report on. Then in Access, click on **Create** and then click on **Report Wizard**. Pick your query and then add the needed fields. Next is the Grouping option. Groups allow you to organize the report based on some category. Excel has this feature as well. It allows you to have totals (actually subtotals) and details in the same place (remember, that was a limitation of queries). Let's take a basic example. Suppose you are in sales and you want to visit customers. You may want to create a report that breaks down your customers by city (so you can better plan your trip). So, when you set up your report, you want to Group on city. You then choose a sort order in the Wizard and a formatting style. Then you finish and there is your report.

Report Design Sections

We will talk more about navigating in the Report Design environment when we talk about Forms. However, designing reports is a bit different in that the **sections** available in Report Design are a bit different.

> *Sections add data and organization to Access Reports or Forms including grouping, subtotals, and grand totals.*

The first section in Report Design is the Report Header section. Any control that you place here will only show once at the very beginning of the report. Normally you use a Label control to simply type the name of the report. You also might want to include a date here. You can do this by using a built-in **function**.

> *A function is a series of instructions (normally calculations) carried out all at once. It is more efficient than carrying out each step separately. You can also pass information (called parameters) that the function uses as part of its calculation.*

To include today's date in your Report Header section, follow these steps:

1. Click on the **Design** menu option.
2. Click once on the **Text Box** control.
3. Move your mouse (normally to the top right portion of the Report Header section).
4. Click to place the Text Box on your report.
5. You don't need the label for the Text Box so deselect the text box by clicking somewhere else in Report Design.
6. Click on the label and hit **Delete** key on keyboard. The label will be removed.
7. Note that this Text Box is unbound since there is no field associated with it. However, we can insert a function that will automatically show today's date.
8. Click once to select the Text Box and click a second time and your cursor will flash inside the Text Box.

9. Type: = **Date()**
10. If you want to format the date, bring up the **Property Sheet** for this control and click on **Format** tab and choose an option under the **Format** property.

The next section in Report Design is the Page Header section. Anything you place here will show on the top of every page of the report. Normally you would place the Label controls here for any fields that you might use in the report. This would tell the user what details they are seeing.

As mentioned earlier, you can also add Groups in Report Design by clicking on the **Design** menu option and then clicking on **Group & Sort**. If you want subtotals, add the Group Footer and Access can insert the calculation you want or you can do it manually (see above example).

The Detail section shows your data so you need Bound controls here. To add a field value, click on **Design** menu and then click on **Add Existing Fields** option. You can then click and drag the fields you want into the Detail section. In some versions of Access, when you place a field in the Design section, it automatically adds the Label in the Page Header. But, you may have to position labels manually.

As you can see, there is wisdom in creating a basic report with the Report Wizard as this will organize and format your data automatically. After the report is completed and saved, then you can go into Report Design to modify as needed.

The Page Footer section prints the same thing at the end of every page. As you have probably noticed, the Page Header and Footer sections in Report Design work basically the same way as headers and footers in Microsoft Word. Normally you would place page numbers at minimum in the Page Footer section. You also might want to place the report name or name of the company. You can also add an unbound Text Box control and enter a function statement. For example, you may want to create a footer that reads: Page 1 of 8

="Page " & [Page] & " of " & [Pages]

Note that we are entering text as part of this expression. *Page* returns the current page number (note brackets around it as a system function). *Pages* gives the total number of pages in the report. The quotation marks indicate that what is inside is text and not a field value. The & is used to combine text (so like an addition sign for text).

The final section in any report is the Report Footer. This is where you place any grand totals for your report. Again, the Report Wizard will automatically enter any grand totals you request in this section. But, you can add calculations (as discussed above) manually if needed. Note that you would use the same expressions (calculations) in the Report Footer as you would use in any Group Footer (where you are getting subtotals). Access will calculate them differently based on the section where the expression occurs.

You can add charts and graphs to Access reports but it is recommended that you export data to Excel and build your charts and graphs using Excel, since it is better suited for this functionality.

Chapter Review

This chapter provided an overview of queries and reports and their application in answering questions. Each type of query was defined and applied. We also covered the use of queries for Transaction processing, MIS, Decision Support, and data management. The fundamentals of building queries were examined and then advanced techniques of record selection and query design were discussed. You should have developed both an appreciation for the power of database queries and a solid foundation for creating and applying queries in a database application system.

Lab

Using the *NorthWind* database, create queries:

1. Create monthly employee sales report.
2. Create a query to show product sales for a certain time period.
3. Initiate a re-order based on checking the *Products* reorder number.
4. Create invoices for customers.

Chapter 5
Capture Data with Forms

Chapter Overview

In this chapter, you will learn important techniques for building forms for working with data. You will start with the basics of user-interface theory. Then, after reviewing the essentials of the Access form design environment, you will learn how to effectively capture and present data in a way that effectively communicates with users.

Goals for Learning

- Understand the basics of user interface theory.
- Understand the importance of communication in database development.
- Understand how to present the data with user-friendly forms.
- How to work efficiently in the form design environment.
- How to name those objects.
- Setting properties.
- Understand how to handle special cases.

Questions to Answer as You Read

1. What are the basics of user interface theory?
2. What does it mean that "communication is important" in database development?
3. How do you create forms?

Terms to Know

Event
Event-driven programming
Record locking
Subform
Tab Order
User interface
User interface design

How We Use Forms

You have a solid database foundation. You have set up your tables and have created the main queries from those tables. As a power user, you could stop there. You have everything you need to store and retrieve meaningful data. But you want to create something that others can easily use. You want to lead them in a clear way into the data that you have so meticulously set up. You want to make sure people enter correct and consistent information so that your queries work properly. You also want your users to work quickly.

Now that you have created the data world, you need to bridge that data world to the real world of your users so that it looks familiar. You do that through the proper use of forms. The key word here is *communication*. You want to set up your forms in a way that clearly *communicates* to your users so that they quickly and easily know what to do and how to do it.

You communicate in two ways. You set up forms to capture data. Here you communicate with the user what you want them to enter and how. You also want them to know how to easily carry out all the activities needed to manage data: adding, editing, and deleting records; and finding needed information and timing of updates in Transaction Processing system applications (this is actually a data action but it has ramifications for the user).

Secondly, you set up forms (and other means) to direct the user to all of the features needed to carry out their work. We will cover this use of these forms in the next chapter.

User Interface Basics

As a Power user, you readily understand that all you need to work with a database is the tables, queries, and reports. You can carry out all of your data management in your tables' Datasheet views. Forms are just a user-friendly way to work with the data. It is kind of like eating a meal. You can cruise through a fast food joint and order food. It is quick but fulfills your basic need for nutrition. But will users be satisfied?

Instead, you can also indulge by going to a fine dining establishment where the waiter greets you warmly and there is soft music playing with freshly cut flowers in a crystal vase on your table. You order a tasty dish and it is served with all the trimmings cooked to perfection. You get the picture. The latter scenario is like using forms; it is a more relaxing and peaceful and satisfying way to work with your information, especially for users.

Now is the time you change hats as an excellent database developer. Up until now, you have focused on the technical side of the work. You might say you have been working *under the hood* of the car on the engine (interestingly enough, the data performance functionality of the database is often called an *engine*). You have created a database structure that the vast majority of users will not understand. You have translated their organizational world into an effective data foundation with accompanying queries. Now it is time to make the transition back to the real organizational world of the user. You have to set up a means of communicating so that the user clearly understands how to get at your data design world and what you need from them to make your data design world happy. You have to get into the heads of your users and try to set up a world on the screen that they will readily understand and be happy with. This requires great skill because initially this requires more psychology than technology (however, obviously, you need technical skill to create the layout that suits). You may have a great data design that accurately reflects the work of the organization, but if people do not know how to get to it or they enter the wrong information then you have a problem. Also, many times if the users do not understand how to work with the world you have set up, they may refuse to use it, so your system goes nowhere (which happens all too many times). We call this area of database development building the **user interface**, or **user interface design**.

A user interface is simply a user-friendly bridge between the organizational activities (real world) and the tables (data design or data world) and queries that reflect those activities. The bridge is normally the forms.

The user interface design is the planned layout of forms to most efficiently and effectively guide users through the application.

If you have read this far in the book, you are concerned about communication in database development. This is one of the key themes of the book. You are receiving the critical information that you need to guide you in working with others to develop consistency in your definitions and your approach to creating databases that support the work of your organization. That is why we covered the material that we covered in the first part of the book. Many organizations fail to benefit from good databases because of a lack of communication.

Forms are arguably the most critical aspect of your database application from the user's perspective. The design of forms makes the difference between people using your data effectively by entering proper information and being able to understand how to find the information they need in a timely way and being totally lost and confused to the point of causing problems.

As mentioned earlier in the book, "back in the day" a developer could program dBase to show a "menu" on the screen when the application "ran." It "waited" for the user to press a key before it did anything. For example, here was a common "menu."

1. Add Customer
2. Edit Customer
3. Delete Customer
4. Customer Report
5. Exit

Type number and press ENTER: ___

Your cursor ended up to the right of *ENTER* and you "worked" the system by typing in the appropriate number and (as instructed) pressing the **Enter** key. This was called *Command-driven programming* where the program dictated what the user must do (like in a Web application for purchasing a book). It was simplistic but users knew exactly what to do. There was little confusion from menus, floating toolbars or popup windows. Basically, at 64K of RAM, your system couldn't handle it! With the advent of the Windows operating system in the late 80s, things began to change. Fox software released a DOS based version of FoxPro in the early 90s that introduced a new approach to database development, called the **Event-driven** approach. This release was ahead of its time in PC database applications.

> *Event-driven programming creates code to react to the actions (called "events") that the user takes.*

This meant that DBMSs had to be set up with **events** that might occur so that code could be applied as desired.

> *An event is something that the user does while using your application. Your routine will respond to this event and run.*

So, Microsoft Access was released shortly thereafter with many capabilities, but still computers were not robust enough to effectively handle these new features from a performance standpoint. The mid 90s showed a transition to using the full features of the Windows environment in real applications, especially with Access 2.0. Since the mid-90s using windows has become the accepted environment for new development. With the increasing capability came more features resulting in more options in database applications. Now you can use menus, toolbars, pictures, and more complicated controls, with really no concern about performance issues.

Web development went through the same transitions due to performance (band-width) constraints. Now things are changing again. With Web development, we are returning to simpler interfaces and moving away from the complexity of an event-driven environment. Perhaps the main driver of this simplicity is sales. You want to make it easy for customers to buy things (i.e. Amazon's *1-click* purchase).

So, the question for developers is: "how do you design a user interface that allows the best balance between clarity of what to do (ease of use for neophytes) and flexibility (maximum efficiency for more experienced users)?" You want to make sure people can use what you have created. The design must meet the needs of the users, not you. It is difficult for you to look at things from their perspective so you must include them early and often in evaluating your work. This inclusion is self-evident. But there is a complication. Not all users are the same. Each user wants their "own" version. So, developers put all kinds of features in software hoping that one "sticks." The result may please one or two users (or even a group) who requested the feature but can confuse other users because of the busyness of the options. Also, the Power user has to put up with these additions to make things *easier* but may take longer to access.

Here are some helpful suggestions adapted from Kelly Doney (2001) of how to accomplish this balance.

- Use storyboard for user interface (should reflect good business processes. If processes are bad, fix them before moving ahead with development). Consider paper forms as objects on the storyboard.
- Make sure the user interface effectively bridges the system world with the business world that users are familiar with.
- Look for good examples and implement usability guidelines that help users understand how to move to where they need to go.
- Use words in interface that are familiar to the user.
- Organize content so it is familiar to users.
- Make sure the look and feel of the user interface is consistent: same menus, similar color scheme, same words.
- Involve users throughout and allow their needs to drive design decisions. If there is any question about what the forms should look like, build a prototype and let the users decide.
- Perform testing early and often to make sure your application works properly with real users. The best way to do this is to watch several different users perform actual tasks with your application. This is the most critical check to ensure that your user interface will work effectively. This can be a daunting task. As someone has said, watching users trying to work with your application is like watching

a horror film. You know they are heading for trouble but you cannot stop them because of the test environment.

- It doesn't hurt to find someone without a computer background to design the look of the forms. You want someone who understands people well and understands the organization so that the interface keeps in mind the people who will actually be using the database.

As you think through the interface, you not only want to consider the look and feel of the forms but also the functionality. By functionality, I mean how the form will work once you open it up. This includes things like: how the cursor moves around in the form when you press the **Tab** key, what mode you are in when you enter the database (whether add, edit or read only), how you work with records (for adding, deleting, editing, and saving), and how you find records.

If an application has a well-designed user interface, a novice user can become productive quickly. The user interface should minimize user errors and provide visual cues to help a user discover how to complete a task. The user of your application should always be in control of the application. This means that procedures should be invoked only when the user invokes them. For example, files should only open or close when the user takes action to open or close them.

Users of your application will have different working styles and different levels of experience working with the application. Therefore, try to accommodate as many levels and styles as possible. For example, do not hard-code colors in your applications. Program your application to use the system colors selected by the user (unless "setting the tone" by using organizational colors, see below).

DO emphasize consistency. The user should not have to relearn information every time he or she uses a new application. The design of the user interface should provide a sense of stability by making the interface familiar and predictable.

Another goal of any interface designer is to create an interface that makes complex tasks simple to perform. Also, be friendly (i.e. with error messages) and provide feedback for a user's actions.

Understand How to Present Your Data with User-Friendly Forms

You are committed to a friendly user interface. Now let's look at specific techniques using Microsoft Access as our tool.

You want a common look for your forms. You want consistency on how to move through forms, where to find menu items and how windows operate. It is helpful, for example, to set up menu items in a way that is similar to what users see in the operating system environment. Try to develop interest in application through design. Use organizational colors; ones that are familiar to the user.

This is where the use of templates is helpful. Once you find a common look for your organization; all your applications should reflect this common look. This is particularly important when you are developing applications for departmental level applications or for small businesses.

Access Form Wizard

Before we discuss how to work effectively in the form design environment, let me comment on the Access templates. When you open Access (in current versions), you will see the different templates such as; *Event Management, Students* and *Services*. You can quickly and easily build these applications. This can give you basic functionality and then you can add to it.

How to Work Efficiently in the Form Design Environment

Here are some steps to keep in mind when setting up a form in the Form Design view:

- Make sure you have first set up the tables in your Access database or attached them. You also set up your queries (if any) that will serve as the Record Source for each form.
- To automatically create a form, click on the data source and the click on **Create** and then click on **Form**. The other option is to simply click on **Create** and then click on **Form Design**. The name of the

form should reflect the entity or business activity that it represents as closely as possible.

- Set the form properties starting with the Record Source property if needed.
- Add the fields to your form.
- Set the properties for each control, especially combo boxes.
- Name your controls using the proper naming conventions.
- Arrange the controls so that they are easy to use: align and set **Tab Order**.

When you are using a form (Form view) in Access, the Tab Order determines where the cursor moves when you press the Tab key.

- Add command Buttons and code for controlling the form.
- Add appropriate menu to form (optional).
- Test and fix as needed.

Now let's work through these steps. As we go through each step, we will discuss in more detail.

Set the Form Properties

Now we are ready to set the form properties. If you let Access create your form, most of the properties are set by the template, but let's review some of the key form property settings. First let's bring up the Form properties window. **Double click** on the black square on form design to bring up the properties of the form. It is just to the left of the top ruler (also above and to the left of the Form Header section of the form design).

If you are designing your form from scratch, you will have to pick the data source by clicking on the **Data** tab of the Form properties window and then click on the Record Source property. Notice that when you click in the Record Source property entry area that a pick list down arrow appears on the far right. This allows you to pick the record source from the tables and queries that are available (list also appears in the Tables and Queries areas of your database window). Determine the table or query that contains the set of fields (and information contained in those fields) that you want to display with the form. Keep in mind that you might have to create a query for the Record Source for this form. Do that before creating the form. Name the query *qryfrmName* where *Name* is whatever the name of the form is. Include the *frm* so that when you look at your list of queries it will be clear that this query goes with the form. Now we will have all of the fields available from the *Company* table to place on the form.

Let's look at a few of the other important Form properties and when you might want to change them. Let's continue on the Data tab of the Form property window. Notice the *Allow* property options: Allow Edits, Allow Deletions, Allow Additions. These three properties determine the mode of the form. By changing these items, you change the default mode that the user faces when entering the form. You also have the option of setting Data Entry to *Yes* which means that users can only enter new records using the form. You can take control of the form using these techniques. As we will see when discussing coding, you can easily change these settings depending on security settings or in response to actions taken by the user. For example, you may not want certain users to change data so you can put the user into data entry mode.

The properties on the **Format** tab help you position the form and control how the user can work with the window which contains the form. Let me go over a few key properties and what they do for you.

- Description: Always include a description for basic objects.
- Caption: This property allows you to type a title for the form that appears in the Window Title when the form is open in form view.
- Default View: You want to set this to Single Form. Often, I set to Continuous Forms when creating forms for lookup tables.
- *Allow* options: These determine whether the user can switch to Datasheet view when working with the form. Often times in departmental level applications I will give the user this ability through a menu item.
- Record Selectors: Normally, you should switch this property to *Yes*. The only two times you may need to select a record is when you want to delete or when you want to copy the record and do a Paste Append (when in Form view, an option under the **Home** menu and

Paste in **Clipboard** section). You can use code or include the Select Record option under the Edit menu to accomplish the same thing.

- Navigation Buttons: These are the small buttons on the bottom left of the form that allow the user to move from one record to the next, add records and see the number of records. With departmental level applications you can leave this on *Yes* but on professional applications you want to turn this off and control movement in other ways.

- Auto Center: I set this to *Yes*. This means that when the form opens in Form View that it will appear in the middle of the screen. This provides consistency for the user.

- Border Style: Normally I leave this on *Thin*. This prevents users from resizing the window. Normally, you do not want users to do this. *Dialog* will also do this.

- Control Box and Close Button: You do not want to show the Control Box or Close Button (set to *No*). You want users to click on some Navigation (or command Button) control to exit the form so that you can control the exit with code. If you show the Control Box (windows close button), you just make more work for yourself. This is the same with Min Max Buttons property. Set to *None*.

Now let's briefly discuss the important properties under the **Other** tab of the Form properties windows.

- Pop Up: A Pop Up is a window that remains on top of other windows even when the window does not have the focus. In every case that I have experienced, I do not want to set Pop Up to *Yes* unless I also set Modal to *Yes*. By setting both of these properties to *Yes*, you set up a Dialogue box and force the user to do something (including simply closing the form) before they exit the form. This can be a helpful technique to prevent users from getting into trouble while using your application.

- Modal: Setting a window to *Modal* means that the form will not lose the focus until you close it. In every case that I have experienced, I do not want to set Modal to *Yes* unless I also set Pop Up to *Yes*.

- Cycle: You want to keep this on *Current Record*. This means that as you tab through the form in Form view that you stay on that record when you press tab on the last control instead of going to the next record. It confuses users when you set this to something besides Current Record.
- Menu Bar: This is where you determine which menu will appear when you use the form in Form view.

Set Control Properties

Now that you are familiar with some of the key properties of the form, let's add our fields to the form so it can work for us. If Access created the form, then the fields are already added. As you may have remembered, we are not actually adding fields to the form but *Bound controls*. The controls are like a window that displays a field value depending on what record you are looking at.

Now, let's set the properties for each control. Each type of control has a different set of properties. In most cases, you do not change control properties once you have set the Control Source (under Data tab) which is set automatically when you drag the field from the field list on to the form in Design view. You do set control properties when naming the control (next topic) and adding code (later in the book). Also, sometimes you may want to override the format for the field (set in data design) by changing the Format property (on Format tab of property window) and sometimes you may want to make a field invisible (set Visible property on Format tab to *No*).

Now let's talk about the control that does require changing properties, the Combo Box control. Once you set up a Combo Box, you need to change several properties to make the control work properly. Let's review the properties you need to change. Remember we are talking about the properties for the Combo Box control only.

- Row Source Type: This property designates the type of data that you will access to fill your pick list. What you choose here will determine what you enter in the Row Source property. As a developer, in all cases you will set this property to Table/Query.

- Row Source: This property is critical because it determines which fields will appear in the Combo Box list that the user will see in Form view. You want to create a query that will show the user enough information to make an accurate choice. This includes at least two fields from the lookup table: The Primary key field and some other field that includes more information. The Primary key should always be the first field in your list. Click on the three dots and you will see a query window. Notice that the title of the query window title bar now says *Query Builder*. Create the query for your pick list but do not save the query. Simply close the window and when it asks you to save the SQL statement click on *Yes*. Now you are back to the properties window and the SQL statement has been added.

- Bound Column: This setting determines which field value from the query will be stored in the field represented by this Combo Box control. You count from left to right. Remember that *Column* is another name for *Field*. That is why you should always put the Primary key as the first field in your list because you want that to be the *Bound Column*.

- Limit To List: The Combo Box control allows users to enter something different from the list. You do not want this. Set the Limit To List property to *Yes*. That means that if users want a different option, they have to update the pick list table before they can use it here. This maintains the integrity of your data.

- Auto Expand: This allows you to type the first few characters of your choice and then Access will bring up one that matches. This is a helpful shortcut when you have a long pick list. With small lists, it will find the correct item. You can also use this technique along with F4 with long lists that contain similar entries. You can type the first two or three letters and then press F4 to open up the list in the area of the list that you need. You can then use **Up** or **Down** arrow key on keyboard to find the exact match and then press **Tab** to keep the choice and move to the next control.

Now let's look at the properties on the **Format** tab of a Combo Box control.

- Column Count: The column count is the number of columns (or fields) contained in the query that serves as your Row Source. Normally you want to show every column from the query unless you are using one column (the last one) for setting Criteria.

- Column Heads: This determines whether or not Column Headings will show on the list that users see when they click on the down arrow of the Combo Box when using the form in Form view.

- Column Widths: This is where you enter the width that you want to reserve for each column when you display data to the user. You use a semi-colon (;) to separate the widths for each column. Normally, you want to make sure there is enough width for each column to display the widest entry to the user. You will have to test the list to make sure you have the right widths for each column in the Combo Box Row Source query. By default, the value of the first column in your query will appear on the form after you make your selection. This will be the Primary key field value. We want that value stored because that is our Foreign key field and allows us to link with the main table for the form. However, this presents a problem because normally the value of this Foreign key field is not easily understood by the user. One way to resolve this problem is to set the Column Width for the first column to 0. This action hides the Primary key field value and lets the user see the meaningful data in the following column(s). But the first column (Foreign key field value) is still bound (see above) so even though you don't see it, the Foreign key field value is what is actually entered into the table.

- List Rows: Enter a number here. This determines how many rows from the Row Source query will appear when the user clicks on the down arrow while in Form view. The user can see additional rows (or Records) by scrolling. Normally I set this to 12.

- List Width: Enter a number here. This determines how wide the list from your Row Source query will be when the user clicks on the down arrow. I recommend that you set this number to the total of the total from the Column Width property settings.

You should set one more property for your control before exiting. Click on the **Other** tab and then click on the **Name** property. A default entry will show (normally whatever the field name is). It is OK to keep the default name but add prefix *cbo*. So, if the field is *CompanyID* and the default control name is also *CompanyID*, you should change the control name to *cboCompanyID*. Now you can exit.

You would apply the same technique (with variations) for the other controls on the form. Make sure to change the name of each control at minimum.

Other Considerations

Now that we have discussed the basics for setting up forms efficiently and effectively, let's look at a few special cases that you might face.

Sometimes you want to hide certain objects on the form and show others. For example, you may want to create one form and show just certain portions of the form depending on the situation. You may tie this to security where you just want certain people using certain parts of the form. Often times, when you use a **subform** you want to include the Foreign key field in the subform so that you can refer to it, but you do not need to show it to the user because the value will normally already appear as the Primary key in the main form.

> *A subform is a form that appears within a form, linked by a common field (or field); normally showing a one-to-many relationship in one place.*

To hide a control on a form, simply change a property setting. Open up a form in Design View and click on any control. Bring up the properties window for that control and then click on the Format tab. Then click on the Visible property and change to *No*.

You need **Record locking** only in a networked situation where you have two or more people trying to change the same record at the same time; which is common in Transaction Processing systems.

> *Record locking follows rules to make sure that only one person is changing the record at a time and that others who are trying*

> *to change know this. Record locking maintains the integrity of*
> *the data in a fair way.*

Think about a scenario. You want to buy tickets to a big basketball game. You go online to buy. Meanwhile, many other people want tickets. You want a procedure (explained later in the book) that does not allow other people (in this case) to "cut in line." If you reserve tickets and start paying for them online, you do not want someone else buying those same tickets when you are buying them. When you try to purchase tickets at 10:05 am, you do not want someone else to take your tickets who comes online at 10:07 am.

You start by setting the form property *Record Locks* (a property under the **Data** tab) to *Edited Record*. If you set to All Records, then no one can access the data in that table when one person is editing; which is probably more control than you need.

Also consider setting up temporary tables for data entry. This will speed things up by avoiding having to open the entire data set when entering information. You can then post the activities at night using an Append Action query. This can also allow you to enter information at different sites and then consolidate the information into one place.

Chapter Review

In this chapter, you learned important techniques for building forms for working with data. To build usable forms, we covered the basics of user-interface theory. Finally, we learned how to effectively capture and present data in a way that effectively communicates with users.

Lab

Using tables from Chapter 3 Lab, create forms for the Training Management System.

Chapter 6
Run Your Application with Forms

We want to now cover the second use of forms, mentioned in chapter 5, setting up forms to direct the user to all of the features needed to carry out their work. We talked about how critical it is to communicate effectively. Laying out forms for data entry entails listening to the user and showing them (via your form design) what they are used to seeing. Now you have to shift gears and use forms to lead the user. You want them to find the items they need to do their work but also you want to set up the order of things so that the user receives what they need when they need it without getting into trouble so that they can be productive for the organization.

You will learn to create forms to direct users through the application. You will also explore cases when you use forms for other special purposes.

Chapter Overview

Chapter 6 shows you how to use Access forms to run applications. You will learn about the importance of application flow. This section will build on the previous chapter and continue the discussion of user-interface theory as it applies to application flow. You will learn how to set up switchboards for automating applications and how to decide the order of flow. The chapter will also cover how to set up other special kinds of forms.

Goals for Learning

- Decide on the application flow.
- Set up switchboards.

Run Your Application with Forms

- Learn special settings.
- Add graphics.
- Add command Buttons.
- Arrange your actions.
- Set up other special forms.

Questions to Answer as You Read

1. What does it mean to *set up the application flow*?
2. What is a switchboard and how do you use it?
3. What is a command Button and how do you use it?
4. What are some other special kinds of forms?

Terms to Know

Application flow
Library
Procedure
Storyboard

Decide on Application Flow

Let's expand our understanding of user interface design to include **application flow.**

> *Application flow is how the user interface (mainly forms) leads the user to the different features of the entire application in order to accomplish required business tasks.*

We will look at what it includes and why it is important. Then we will discuss how to set up the application flow.

Understand Application Flow

Application flow is the next important step in allowing users to get their work done. When users open a database application, they are presented with several different options. Users have expectations that they will be able to accomplish their work by using the database application. You might say that there is trust involved. Users trust you as the developer to show them where to go. It is like there is a dark night and the power just went off, and you have a flash light. They need you to show them the way in the midst of the darkness so they know where to go. As the developer or one who manages a development project, you need to be sensitive to these expectations (as much as possible) of users.

But there is another aspect to application flow. Along with the trust, is a "creative" spirit where users want to go wherever they want to go despite the business processes. So, part of your work is to serve the business interests by keeping people on task. Here the application flow creates effective walls to prevent users from wandering off task and getting into trouble. You ultimately help the user do the work but you also protect the goals of the process which is to streamline work. These two purposes can create tension when trying to set up a database application. The way to resolve the issue is to be honest and open about what you are doing and, as you know, test thoroughly.

The application flow is important because it must reflect the business process (or processes) that the database supports. It is imperative that the user can quickly and easily move through the different features of the application. To ensure that this happens, you need to think it through.

Set Up the Application Flow

Now we want to set up the application flow. How do we want people to work with our database application? Keep in mind that throughout your database development, that these three things should be in synch:

1. Process diagram (real work world);
2. Data flow diagram (how your data design reflects the real world);
3. Application flow (which should tie together the business process that the user is familiar with and the data world in a seamless way).

So, when you make changes to one, you make changes to the others. For example, as you are setting up the application flow, you might find that there is a gap in the process that needs to be fixed. You then make sure data and any other objects are adjusted to reflect this change.

So, what is the best way to set up the application flow? You can probably find any number of approaches, but we will focus on one that I recommend in this book (and touched on last chapter); the **storyboard** approach.

> A storyboard is a set of graphics in order to represent "scenes" in a movie, for example, or layout steps in database applications or websites.

Storyboards are used in the film industry to set up the flow of a movie. It uses pictures to reflect scenes in the film and the order of those scenes. This technique is helpful because you can then place the entire storyboard on a wall or chart and look at it and make sure that there are no gaps in the story. The PowerPoint **Slide Sorter** view does the same kind of thing.

When it comes to database development, this visual approach makes sure that users know where to go in the application. It particularly makes sure that the transitions are clear and the verbal and visual cues to guide users are easily understood. This also insures that the database flow accurately reflects how the work moves forward in the organization.

Set Up Switchboards

Now we are ready to design our special forms. First let's look at switchboards. A *switchboard* is a term that Microsoft coined to describe a menu that appears on a form (as mentioned in earlier in the book). They also use the term *navigation form*. It alludes to a switchboard like on a train system where it directs trains to specific tracks and locations or like in an electrical system where it channels electricity from a switch to a particular light fixture. The whole idea is that a switchboard organizes and directs activity so nothing is lost and actions are completed properly.

Because of the windows environment, you can place direction options on a switchboard form as well as have menu options at the top of screen. You can also add ribbons (at the top of the screen) or toolbars (which can *float*) to also make commands available. Let's start with the switchboard, but you can add commands in similar ways to menus or ribbons or toolbars. Here are the steps for setting up your switchboard: learn special settings, add graphics, add (command) Buttons, and arrange your actions.

Switchboard Form Property Settings

Go ahead and create a new **Form Design**. Let's start by looking at the data properties. In the properties window, click on the tab that says **Data**. The basic point to make here is that there will not be any Record Source. The switchboard is simply a place to put (command) **Buttons** that activate code to direct the user to different parts of the application. With that out of the way, let's click on the **Format** tab.

Let's examine in more detail the **Format** properties for this switchboard form.

- Caption: Change to *Main Switchboard*. This will appear on the switchboard form window when in form view.
- Default View: You want your main switchboard to open up in *Single Form* view, not Datasheet or Continuous Forms.
- Views Allowed: You do not want the user to be able to switch views on a switchboard so this is set to *Form only*.
- Scroll Bars: You do not want any scroll bars on a switchboard so this is set to *Neither*.
- Record Selectors: This is set to *No* because you have no records to select since there is no Record Source to the form.
- Navigation Buttons: Again, this is set to *No* because you have no records to navigate to since there is no Record Source to the form.
- Auto Resize: You want the switchboard to maintain a common size based on how you set it up so you want to set this to *No*.
- Auto Center: Set this to *Yes*. You normally want the Switchboard to appear in the middle of the screen each time.
- Border Style: Keep this on *Thin*. This prevents the user from resizing the window. You do not want to change the size of this window.
- Control Box: Set to *No* because you do not want the user to close the main switchboard manually. You want them to exit by using a menu option or command button.

- Min Max Buttons: Again, you do not want users to minimize or maximize the main switchboard. Set this property to *No*.
- Close Button: Set to *No*. This is so users can't "lose their guide." But you do want to give them an **Ex̱it** button (with code that exits the application when the user clicks on it) to get out of the application.

Let's look at one more property tab for the form before we move on. Click on the **Other** tab and let's look at four property settings here.

- Pop Up: Set his property to *No*. We don't want the switchboard form to remain on top of other windows.
- Modal: Set this property to *No*. We do not want this form to retain the focus until closed. We want to hide the main switchboard as we go through our application and this must be set to No to allow this movement.
- Cycle: Set to *Current Record*. If the user wants to tab through the switchboard, then this will keep them on this form. This is particularly important since there are no other records to go to. (NOTE: I recommend that you set this property to *Current Record* on any form.)
- Menu Bar: This is where you indicate the menu that you want to appear when the form opens in form view. Right now, leave this blank. You can develop the menus later. The same applies to the **Toolbar** and **Ribbon Name** properties. You do not want to activate your menus until the very last. Otherwise, it makes development in form design view unwieldy. We will add menus to all the forms later on.

That's it for the properties. Save your changes by clicking on the **File** menu and choosing **Save**. Now you are ready to add any desired graphics to the main switchboard.

Switchboard Form Graphics

Part of setting up the switchboard is to create a user-friendly atmosphere and let the user know that they are welcome and that this *database application world* is familiar. You want to set up a look that is professional, clear, and makes the user feel that this application is not something foreign but there to make their work easier. This is particularly critical when the application is new (change management situation) and you are trying to coax your people into changing to this different (but better) approach.

Adding a crisp picture that captures your business can prove helpful to users. It also helps you build your organizational culture by encouraging the user with organizational principles and slogans. Let's examine how this might look.

Feel free to open the switchboard that we just discussed or just create a new **Form Design**. Click on the Image control on the Design ribbon and then click on your form. It will ask you for a file. Simply click on the graphic file you want to use. You can then resize and position the graphic on the form.

You can change the graphic if you like. Open up the properties for the Image control and click on the **Format** tab. Now click on the Picture property. When you click inside the Picture property, you will see the three dots (…). Click on the three dots and the Insert Picture window will appear, which allows you to insert a different graphic.

Now that we have the Properties window open, let's take a brief look at some of the other Property options for this Image control.

- Picture: As mentioned, this is where you designate the location of the graphics file that you want to place into the image control.
- Picture Type: The two options here (from pick list that appears when you click into the property area) are Linked or Embedded. An Embedded picture stays with the Access database file. Choosing this option will ensure that the picture goes with the database when you install or copy the database file. However, it makes your database bigger. The Linked option places a pointer so that Access loads the file when the form is open. This may take slightly longer. Also, if you happen to move the reference graphic file, then Access will not be able to display the graphic. I recommend that you Embed when setting up a switchboard, however when you are storing graphic data in an OLE Object datatype field, consider Linking.
- Size Mode: This property allows you to determine how the picture will appear in the Image control area reserved for it (or picture

frame you might say). Again, you see a pick list (black down arrow) when you click into this property. You have three options here: *Clip*, *Stretch*, and *Zoom*. Normally, you want to choose the Zoom option. This keeps the picture in the frame for the picture (as determined by the Image control area) so that you do not have to change the layout of the form. It also keeps the proportions of the picture. The Clip option presents the picture according to its original size which may or may not (almost always not) fit into the Image control frame for the graphic. The Stretch option makes the graphic fill up the Image control frame area but usually distorts the picture in the process (it loses its proportion).

- Picture Alignment: Usually you want to set this property to *Center*. You are normally concerned about the layout of the entire form and the position of the Image control on that form (whether left, right, or center). Once you have positioned the Image control, you normally want to keep the picture within the control centered. But you do have four other options.
- Picture Tiling: This option allows you to repeat the picture within the Image control. Normally you would set this to *No* unless you want to create an effect by having several copies of the graphic, which will appear as you make the control wider.

Now that we inserted the desired picture in our Image control, let's discuss Buttons. Continue in **Design View**. Click once on the Button control and then move your mouse to the form and click again to place the button. Notice that after you click to add the Button, and depending on what version of Access you have, you may see a Wizard option pop up which gives you commands that you can add. For now, just hit **Cancel**.

When working with code, it is best to set up a **library** that contains code for the basic things that you do with your database.

A library (called module in Access) is a group of programs in one place that you can use anywhere in the application; and can be stored in the same database or a different one.

You can then simply refer to the code in the library when you add code to the event in your forms that run the application.

Adding code to forms is a three-step activity:

1. You find the object that you want to work with and open up the properties for that object.
2. You click on the **Event** tab in the properties window and select the proper event for your code.
3. You add the code to that event. In our case, this means typing in a name that refers to the code in our library.

For example, suppose you have a **procedure** that opens up a form. So, when the user clicks on this command Button, the form will open.

> *A procedure (also called a "program") is a specific set of code that accomplishes some task or calculates a value. It is a small program that has a distinct focus. Procedures are common in Event-driven programming. A procedure can also be called a "routine."*

Open up the Properties for the command Button. Click on the **Event** tab on the properties window. Click in the *On Click* event. We want code to execute when the user clicks on this Button. We want to open up (for example) the *frmCompany* that is part of our database. In our example, suppose we have a procedure in a Library called *OpenMyForm* which requires a form name as a parameter. Then we would type this in the On Click event: *=OpenMyForm("frmCompany")*

Let's briefly discuss this statement. The = (equal sign) is required because we are referring to a certain style of code in our library. The *OpenMyForm* is the name of the piece of code we are referring to in our library. This piece of code allows you to tell it the name of the specific form that you want to open. In our case, we want to open the *frmCompany* that is part of this database.

Set Up Forms to Pick Options

The main switchboard is the control center for your application. It directs your people to where they need to go to accomplish their work in the proper way at the proper time. However, there are times when people need to use a different type of form to pull up information: in order to find an individual item or group of items, in order to set criteria for a report, or in order to pick options from a list. Let's discuss these situations in this next section.

As you know by now, you create and use a query to pull up a certain set of information that you need to do your work. However, creating queries requires a certain level of knowledge (especially in how to set the needed criteria) that is not available to novices (the main group of people using your application). You want to be able to set up user-friendly forms that allow your users to enter criteria that goes to your query to give the proper results which can then be shown in a report (if needed).

We want to create a form to set criteria that will be passed to the query that serves as the Data Source for our report. Basically, you go into Form Design and add, for example, a List Box control that refers to types of projects. Then you want to add a command Button that runs the report (and underlying query) based on the selection the user makes in the List Box. After setting up your form, refer to the form value in your query criteria. Suppose your form name is *afrmrptProjectType*. Note the prefix (*a*), designating that this is an action form and that the form is tied to a certain report so refers to report name as well. Let's say that the name of the List Box control is: *lstProjectType*. The query serving as the data source for the report would be: *qryrptProjectType*. So, you would go to the query and enter the following as the selection criteria for the *ProjectType* field:

Forms!afrmrptProjectTypeSelect!lstProjectType

The Build option can help you with this syntax if needed.

Although this technique is useful, it can never meet all of the requirements users might have for how they want to look at the data. If you are developing a departmental level application or an application for a small office, it is often not worth the time to try to create application forms for all the different options users might desire. Also, you will find that you may never meet their needs. It is better to set up the basic selection options (for transaction processing or management information needs) in this user-friendly way but also train power users who can learn to understand the data design for the application (why you need a good and understandable Data Dictionary), understand how to write basic queries, and then learn to write basic reports using those queries (mainly for decision support requirements). This will give users maximum flexibility in using the data. Power users should set up a separate database for these ad hoc queries and reports and then attach to the data files. Then the ad hoc items do not clutter the main application. If the power users develop an ad hoc query and report that becomes consistently useful, then it can be easily added to the main application as a menu item.

Understanding Menus

Now that we know more about running your application, let's discuss menus. Menus provide you with another option for making things happen. But when and how do you use menus effectively?

Menus differ from switchboards in that they appear at the top of the screen and you can use them on other forms and reports. Switchboards are constrained because they are single forms. You can return to the form any time but it is the same form.

Menus and switchboards are the same in that you can run VBA code (or a macro) from each. However, they are different in how you execute the code. With menu options, the code runs when you pick the menu option. With switchboards, the code runs when you click on the command Buttons that appear on the switchboard.

Why use menus? Access is replete with ways to make things happen in your application. We have just covered switchboards and how the user can click on command Buttons to do everything needed to carry out work. We have not discussed toolbars or ribbons; which are other ways to make things happen. Let's examine why menus are distinctive and how they can contribute to your database application functionality.

Menus are useful in two important ways. They allow you to make common actions easily available to users. For example, on every form, you may want users to be able to do the following: call up the Access Find action, Exit the application, or switch between Datasheet and Form views. You can set up a menu that can perform these actions. You can then apply that common menu to each and every form. This gives flexibility and continuity to your application.

Secondly, you want to use menus to run actions that might be destructive to the data; like Delete. If the Delete option is available as a command button on a form, it is too easy to click and delete without thinking. You can add a check to the delete action through code but moving the action off of the form to a menu item gives you another level of protection. This holds true for running any Action query.

Toolbars work the same way as menus except they appear in a different format. For small development projects, I don't recommend toolbars because they add to the busyness of an application. Also, toolbars require much programming to make sure that toolbar items do not interfere with other things that are going on in your application. Toolbars also defeat the purpose of menus which is to make things less readily available.

Chapter Review

We covered the second use of forms, setting up forms to direct the user to all of the features needed to carry out their work. You learned how to set up switchboards for automating applications and how to decide the order of flow. The chapter also covered how to set up other special kinds of forms.

Lab

Set up a switchboard form and Buttons for opening the other forms in the Learning Management System.

Chapter 7
Tie Your Application Together with Code

Chapter Overview

Get ready to take your database knowledge to a whole new level. Earlier in the book, we discussed the different people who use Microsoft Access or other database programs. As you remember, a database developer is one who can create an entire application that is easy for others to use. The previous sections prepared you for this next step. This chapter will give you the secrets of how to tie together your application in a more flexible way. We illustrate this by discussing macros and looking at the differences between using macros and Visual Basic for Applications (VBA).

We cover VBA by giving more detail about Event-driven programming, the approach VBA uses. The purpose of the chapter is NOT to tell you everything about Microsoft VBA but to help you understand basic techniques that you can use over and over to build useful database applications. Once you master the principles from this chapter, you can easily expand your knowledge with particular facts about VBA (or another programming language that you might use) as you face particular programming challenges.

Goals for Learning

- Learn about Event-driven programming and how this approach ties to the psychology of the user.
- Cite some of the key events in Microsoft Access.
- Learn how to add actions to switchboards.

- Cite basic commands and how to use them.
- Compare and contrast using macros versus using VBA for your coding.

Questions to Answer as You Read

1. What is Event-driven Programming? What is one key perspective to keep in mind when deciding which events to utilize?
2. List and explain four basic objects and types of events and when you might use them.
3. What are some basic commands that you can use as part of your macro?
4. What are three options you might use to tie together your application?
5. What is a module and how should you use them with VBA?
6. What is the difference between macros and Visual Basic for Applications (VBA)?

Terms to Know

Class module
Code
Declaring a variable
Event procedure
Function procedure
Macro
Method
Module
Standard module
Sub procedure
Visual Basic for Applications (VBA)

Application Development Overview

A goal of the book is to provide an approach to database development that you can use with any database platform, including client-server.

Obviously different platforms require different specifics but overall the principles we have covered in this book will be the same.

Now we are ready to lace together the elements that we have already set up: a solid database design, the queries and reports to pull needed information, user-friendly forms that people can follow, and forms that tie together the entire application. Now it is time to talk specifically about how to set up **macros** or **VBA code** to complete the process. You might say that we have all of the parts to our database puzzle defined and laid out; now we just need a neat way to interlock the pieces into a unified whole.

> *A macro is taking several (micro) steps that you would normally do manually and running them all at once.*

> *Visual Basic for Application (VBA) is the programming language that comes with Microsoft Office products including Microsoft Access. It is a variation of Visual Basic and is useful because it is user friendly, yet powerful.*

> *The code (or lines of code) is the individual lines of instruction that make up a procedure or a program. It is like a sentence (code) in an entire book (the program). These may also be called "statements."*

There are certain principles to apply when approaching database development with Microsoft Access. First of all, you need to determine how robust you want to make the application. For many purposes, you can simply use macros. They are fairly straightforward to create and give your application a user-friendly feel. You can create macro libraries of similar purpose to keep your work organized. Also, macros can be used in a similar way as code. For example, you can use macros with menu selections and as the responses to clicks on command Buttons on forms.

Both macros and VBA respond to events in the database application. So, before we go into more detail about our responses to events, let's spend a little time understanding the events themselves.

If you do not run your macros or code with the correct event (at the right time) in the application, you will have problems. In this section, we'll examine the role (psychology) of the user in Access application development and then discuss common events and how to tie the events to the application flow.

We have already discussed the psychology of the user when we covered form design. Event-driven programming could also be called (in most cases) *user-driven programming*. Think about it (once again!). If your application depends on what the user does, then you better be sure that you think about what you want your user to be able to do or not do. The more you try to respond to any user activity, the more involved the programming. So, you need to get into the head of the user and try to predict what they will do and then plan appropriate responses to those events. One approach to controlling this potential complexity is to limit what the user can do. This allows quicker development and also limits the problems the user can get into. One specific way to limit what the user can do is to NOT use ribbons or toolbars but use menus and command Buttons on forms to guide the user through the application. Having toolbars open everywhere in the application, for example, requires more programming to take them into account; which complicates the application and could lead to problems for the user. You can avoid these potential problems by leaving them out. But if you do want to create toolbars, like menus, consider using different ones for different parts of your application.

Know Your Events

Here are some recommendations of objects and corresponding events to know. These recommendations are meant to help you *walk the line* between giving too many or too few options to users. Hopefully, walking this fine line will make your application development more efficient while still giving users options. To help you prioritize, here are four basic objects and types of events that you should know:

1. Mouse clicks and keystrokes: Events that occur when the mouse button is pushed down or clicked and when keys are pushed.
2. Forms: Events that occur when working with an entire form; like opening and closing the form.
3. Controls on a form: Events that can occur with controls on a form like when a user enters, exits or changes a data value associated with that control.

4. Reports: Events that occur when a report is printed.

Now let's examine these different categories in more detail and look at specific events that are commonly used in basic application development. This list will certainly not be comprehensive. However, it will make you familiar with the events that are most common and, more importantly, will let you know when they are most commonly used.

Mouse Clicks and Keystrokes:

- On Click: Use with command Button on a form to run a procedure; probably the most commonly used event.

Forms:

- On Open: Run when form opens. For example, you may want to go to a certain control when the form opens.
- Before Update: Use to check validity of data before values in controls are written as data to the table.
- On Delete: Run if a record is deleted.
- Before Insert and After Insert: Run before or after a new record is added.
- Dirty: Run when data has changed.

Controls on a form:

After Update: Use to make changes to other data based on what is entered. For example, on a customer form, you might have a Check Box control that says *Shipping address same as credit card address*. So, after checking this box, the address information is automatically copied into the shipping address controls.

Reports:

On No Data: Run when the report has no data results. This allows a smooth way to let the user know that there is no data, so avoids just showing the user a system error.

Tying Access Events to The Application Flow

Now, how do you tie your events to the switchboards and other special forms? You basically take the code or macro that you want to run when the event occurs and tie it to the event. As we have discussed, events for an object are found in the properties for that object. So, to tie the code or macro to an event, you decide which object (usually a form or control on a form) has the event that you are interested in; then open up the properties for that object and find the event property that you want to react to; and then you tie one of three options (see below) to the proper event property. Keep in mind that you can also use macros or code to respond to events that are not directly related to the application flow but for our purposes, this is the main way that we will learn about them.

So, what are three options you might use to tie together your application? You can:

1.   Run a macro,
2.   Run a procedure that is stored in a VBA **module**, or
3.   Run a procedure that is tied to the object where the event occurs.

> *A module is a collection of procedures in one place which makes it easier to manage. You might say that a module is a library that contains a group of procedures.*

Before we talk briefly about macros (our first of the three options), let's examine a basic framework for VBA Modules to use to tie together your application. This is your set of instructions in our Blueprint on how to glue all the pieces together to form a beautiful piece of furniture. These action items apply whenever you are using code.

Set up three libraries (VBA Modules):

1.   one for basic functions that you want to use over and over in all parts of your application (which we will call *basLibrary*).
2.   one for the menu items (which we will call *basMenu*).
3.   one for error checking (which we will call *basErrorHandler*).

Basic Macro Commands to Run Your Application

It is beyond the scope of this book to discuss macros and VBA in detail. However, as a business leader, it behooves you to know something about how a database application can be set up for your users. Keep in mind that when you, for example, add a command Button to a form, the Access Command Button Wizard automatically pops up and allows you to apply an action to the On Click event for that Button. After you complete the Wizard, Access actually generates VBA code using the third option mentioned above: *Run a procedure that is tied to the object where the event occurs*. This is probably the easiest way to tie together your application.

You can create and save macros by using the **Create** menu option in Access and then choosing **Macro**. Note than you can simply add the actions you want the macro to take. For example, you may simply want to show a MessageBox to let the user know something. Or, you can use OpenForm to open a form or use OpenQuery to run a query. Then you can save the steps and give them a name. When you open up the form properties in your form design (for example) and click on the **Event** tab, you will see the macros you created in the pick list.

You can also use macros in your application. Remember that macros can execute several actions all at once. Becoming familiar with macro actions helps you understand some of the actions you can run using code.

Here are some basic macro commands (called Actions or commands) that are available and what they can do for you. Keep in mind that these macro actions also have properties (unique to each action), called *Arguments* which you should complete.

- CloseWindow: Closes the current window (form). You can also close a different window if you run the SelectObject command first and then the CloseWindow command. Use this action with a RETURN command button on a form to close the current form which allows you to return to a main switchboard (as long as it is still open).
- GoToControl: Moves the cursor to a particular control on a form (or field in datasheet view). This command is useful for putting the

cursor exactly where you want it and thus guide users in where they need to be in the program and what they need to do.

- GoToRecord: Goes to a certain record. Set Record property to New to add a record. Use this option instead of Data Entry (from Record menu) which allows you to ONLY enter records and removes you from rest of data.

- MsgBox: As mentioned above, displays a dialogue box that gives a message to the user. This is very helpful whenever you are not sure that the user knows what to do. You can simply "stop" everything, get the user's attention via a dialogue box, and tell them what is going on.

- OpenForm: As mentioned above, opens a form. This is the command you will want to execute when clicking on the command buttons on a main switchboard to open up forms for your application.

- OpenReport: Opens a report. This is the command you will want to execute when clicking on the menu options to open up the reports for your application. Normally, it is recommended that you open up reports in Print Preview mode (View property set to PrintPreview).

- OpenQuery: As mentioned above, runs a query. You will use this occasionally to pull up information for the user. Also, this is the action you will use to run Action queries.

- QuitAccess: Exits Access. Use this command to leave your application and close Access. Normally you will create a command button on your main switchboard that allows the user to Quit or Exit.

- Requery: Requeries a query or table that is a data source for a control. You must put the name of the control in the Control Name property for this action Normally you use this with your Find a record pick list control after you add or delete a record so that your pick list will reflect the change.

- RunCode: Runs a VBA Function. If you use macros to set up your menus and still want to use VBA, then all of your menu options will include RunCode options.

- RunMenuCommand: Perhaps the most powerful macro action available. This option makes available all of the menu commands in Microsoft Access. Click in the **Command** property to see pick list of all the options available. You can use this option, for example, to delete a record (DeleteRecord) or save a record (SaveRecord).

- SelectObject: Selects another object (set **Object Type** property and **Object Name** property). Use this option to go back to the main switchboard (if hidden) after closing the current form.
- ShowAllRecords: Removes a filter. Sometimes you may want to use the RunMenuCommand macro action to call the AdvancedFilterSort menu option. Use the ShowAllRecords option to remove the filter.
- ExportWithFormatting: Exports data. Very useful for sending data to a Word mail merge file or to Excel.

There are some macro actions that may appear useful but do not work as you imagine. For example, there is a FindRecord action which looks useful for locating data. But this command is better suited for working with recordsets in VBA or SQL. You are better off bringing up the **Find...** (CTRL F) dialogue box which will give the user more flexibility in finding things. The macro action that you want to use is: **RunMenuCommand** and then choose the **Find** command.

Macros Versus VBA

It is helpful to have an understanding of macros but using them is a bit confusing in Access. It is better for database developers to have a basic understanding of code (options 2 and 3 mentioned above for tying together your application), when to use it, how to use it, and what it can do for you.

Basically, VBA is much more versatile. Macros are limited to the commands in the list in the macro design view environment. VBA gives you access to the entire Microsoft Office (and Windows) program objects. As mentioned, VBA has robust error checking capabilities which are not available with macros. This keeps your user from getting into trouble.

VBA is a true programming language and has all the techniques available in a programming language like looping and branches. You have a minimal branching capability with macros but that's it. VBA gives you total power to handle any programming problem.

Also, VBA allows you to set up and reuse code over and over and still gives flexibility. For example, macros normally require that you create separate macros for each form that you might want to open in your application. This gets a bit tedious. In VBA, you can simply create a function in a module with a variable (also called *parameter*) defined which allows you to simply pass the form name each time the code is run. This allows you to have one place for this functionality.

VBA Essentials

You understand macros and Event-driven programming. Now you are ready to take the next step to VBA. You want more power and complete control of the user environment. You can read entire books and take complete courses on VBA. This section is certainly not exhaustive but gives you the essentials for building complete Access applications. We will start by going over some basic principles and then spend the rest of the chapter going over different techniques. Let's dig in!

VBA Overview

In the early days (early 1990s) of Microsoft Access (primarily with version 2.0), the product came with a feature called Access Basic. This was a variation of Microsoft's Basic programming language (NOTE: actually, Basic was the product that started Microsoft). Access Basic did not take up a great deal of RAM and was designed to work efficiently in the database environment. In the mid-1990s, Microsoft introduced VBA (Visual Basic for Applications) to all of their Microsoft Office products (actually Excel came first followed by Word and then PowerPoint) including Access. The language allowed a common environment for all the Office products but could be said to be a setback for Access efficiency. Now because of the speed of modern PCs, the performance of VBA has smoothed out. So, let's look at VBA. The good news is that if you can learn something about VBA, you can learn principles that will apply to any programming language (like Java). Also, if you understand something about VBA, you will truly be on your way to becoming a database expert.

VBA is based on Set theory in mathematics. You have objects (which we have discussed earlier). Each object has collections of other objects and a collection of **methods**.

Methods are actions that you can take with on an object or actions that the object can do. It is like a procedure that has already been written as part of VBA.

For example, one method for a table object is the ability to insert new records. You could say that methods are procedures that come with VBA so that you don't have to write them. For example, you have a horse. The horse is the object. The horse can do things (methods) like; trotting, running or eating.

VBA Coding

It is beyond the scope of this book to cover coding exhaustively. However, we will cover the key fundamentals that can be used to build any application. You can then expand your knowledge as you learn more commands and techniques in order to solve specific problems that come up in your work. So, you might say we have the house foundation and framing (the essentials) completed. You just have to add the wall paper and other decorations that you like. There is also the hope that you can take these techniques and information and apply not only for VBA but for any other programming language that you might want to use.

When writing code, you want to keep three points in mind;

1. Make the code easy to follow.
2. Make it clear what the code is doing so it is easier to fix problems and it is easier for someone else to understand what you are doing when you want to add functionality.
3. Reuse code. Try to create modules (libraries) that contain routines that are easily used many times in the current application and for future applications.

Standard Modules Versus Class Modules

As discussed earlier, you can enter your code (produce procedures) in two locations. **Standard** modules are the ones you create and you find them when you click on the Database Window and then click on the **Modules** tab.

> *A Standard module contains procedures that are not associated with any particular object and can be run anywhere within your database.*

Class modules are associated with objects like a form or a control.

> *A Class module contains procedures that run in response to certain events associated with the object; a form or report.*

A more advanced ability of Class modules is that you can use them to create a custom object with associated properties and methods.

Using Standard modules is helpful for two important reasons.

1. It makes your coding quicker. You only have to write one routine instead of a number of routines based on the number of forms you are using (as alluded to above).
2. It organizes your information so procedures are easier to find. If there is a problem, you can correct it in one place (in your Standard module) rather than having to go a number of places (for each Class module instance).

The key question to answer when deciding to use a Standard module for a procedure is: is this functionality repeatable? In other words, are you only creating this code one time for a particular object or are you going to use it again either in this application or in other applications? If the code is truly unique for this object, then *yes*, you should create an **Event procedure** for the code. If not, consider creating a procedure in a Standard module.

> *An event procedure is a particular procedure that runs in response to a certain event attached to an object in a form or report.*

Normally, you want to group our VBA procedures into modules. Access uses a different name for *library*, which it calls a *module*. Historically a *library* has referred to code that many different applications can refer to. In an Access application, everything in the Access database can refer to any procedure in any module (so same as a library). Technically you can put all your procedures (can also be called *routines*) into one module, but it is helpful for organizational purposes to use different modules (as mentioned above). VBA applies an environment to allow you to find things but, it can be cumbersome and confusing so better to group into modules.

Functions Versus Subs

When you create a procedure for an object (which appears in a Class module for that object), you automatically create a **Sub** type of procedure.

A Sub is a procedure that completes some task and does not accept variables.

Microsoft used to call all routines *functions* which was confusing since one type of function was a Function! Fortunately, they are now called *Procedures* and there are two types; Sub (defined above) and **Functions**.

A Function is a procedure that does accept variables. It also can refer to the results of calculation that returns a value.

When you create a procedure for an object which appears in a Class module for that object, you automatically create a Sub procedure.

Just to clarify, Standard modules can contain Sub or Function procedures. To call (or run) a Sub procedure from another procedure, simply type the name of the Sub. For example, suppose you have created a Sub procedure called *CheckData* that checks the validity of data on a certain form and you want to refer to the procedure when you click on the *Save* command button (called *cmdSave*). Your code in the Event procedure would look like this:

```
Sub cmdSave_Click()
        CheckData                'Runs the Sub procedure CheckData
End Sub
```

Subs or Functions always start with the name of the Sub or Function; the code; and then an End (Sub or Function) statement (for example, see above where the procedure ended with the *End Sub* statement).

Let's look at another example. You might create a Function procedure like this which you would put in your module *basLibrary*:

```
Function OpenMyForm(strMyForm As String)      'Add form name.
        DoCmd.OpenForm strMyForm        'Open appropriate form
End Function
```

Note that since we have declared the strMyForm as a String variable, we have to add quotation marks (used with text) around the form name when we apply this Function in an event. Also, whether a Sub or Function, the procedure name is always followed by parenthesis.

As we discussed, a Function has the ability to accept variables (or pass parameters). In the above code example, we are passing the name of a form as a string. This gives the code much flexibility. Instead of having to write this code as a Sub procedure in a Class module for a form you want to open, you can simply refer to it in your event and pass the appropriate name of the form. For example, if you want to open up the company form when you click on the Company button on the *Main Switchboard* form, you can simply type the following into the On Click Event:

=OpenMyForm("frmCompany")

You are telling Access that you want to run the *OpenMyForm* Function when the user clicks on that command button. You can repeat this statement any time you want to open a form by just changing the name of the form that you want to open. This simplifies your coding and it also can improve performance. A form will respond more quickly if you do not have to create a Class module (created automatically when you create a procedure for an object) that goes with it.

Understanding and Using Variables

Each module can contain procedures and what are called declarations (short for **declaring variables**).

Declaring a variable is when you name the variable and give it a type (such as Text or Numeric or Form) at the beginning of a procedure or as part of the name of the procedure.

See our above example where we declared a string variable with our *OpenMyForm* Function. As mentioned above, variables give your code flexibility and power. The value comes from something you enter when you run a Function or that you pass from some other part of the application, such as a number, a field value from a table or a control value that is stored on a form. A variable needs to be declared before it can be assigned a value. Declaring a variable looks something like this in VBA code:

Dim strFormName as String

Note that *strFormName* is the name of the variable and *String* is the type of variable. You normally attach a prefix to your variable name that coincides with the type of variable you are creating. You make variable declarations at the beginning of your Function procedure or as part of the Function name. Remember our example above when you added an action to the OnClick event of a command Button:

=OpenMyForm("frmCompany")

OpenMyForm is a function and we are passing a variable value when running the Function procedure. In naming our function procedure *OpenMyForm*, we have defined a variable called *strMyForm*. When we run the procedure, we are telling it to open a specific form called "*frmCompany.*" Because we are using a variable as part of this procedure, we have maximum flexibility. As we have noted, we can run this same function over and over and simply provide a different form name each time.

VBA Techniques

Now you have a basic understanding of how VBA code works. We have already started talking about some VBA techniques. Let's continue and analyze the tools you have at your disposal to write VBA code.

Referring to Objects

Let's look at some common objects. Most of VBA involves making changes to objects or doing some processing using methods. Just keep in mind that you first refer to the collection then the object in the collection. For Access, it is best to check the **Help** file for syntax (or even the Builder). The benefit of working with objects is that objects provide code that you do not have to write. You simply set the object's properties and call the object's methods. As mentioned previously, methods are *built-in programs* that come with the object. You might call these commands *traffic cops* since they can direct the flow of the application.

To understand the relationship between objects, properties, and methods, consider a stereo radio. The radio is an object and has a number of properties, such as volume, bass, and treble. The radio's volume is a property that you can change. You can also change the radio station, another property, by using the radio's *tune* method. Each of these properties and methods perform a specific purpose and are used to attain a given goal or objective, such as tuning the radio. As a radio owner, you learn how to use these objects, but for the most part, you do not learn how to install, maintain, or repair them. You only need to know how to operate them and what to expect. In the same way, Visual Basic lets you use objects such as forms and controls to build applications. For the most part, you can use objects without having a detailed understanding of how they work.

Branching

VBA provides several ways to control program flow and execution. Conditional statements make it possible for your program to selectively perform tasks based on values generated by your program or by the user. Looping statements contain blocks of code that execute repeatedly until stopped.

The first one decides which fork to take in a road. This is a simple *If... Then* statement. In other words; *If* something is *True*, then run some code. You can then do nothing at that point or run some other code if the condition is *False*.

In general, you use an *If...Then* statement when an *either/or* decision must be made. When your program must select from more than one alternative, use one of the other coding options. There are six operators that you can use in the condition portion of the *If...Then* block:

1. = (Equal),
2. < > (Not equal),
3. < (Less than),
4. <= (Less than or equal to),
5. > (Greater than),
6. >= (Greater than or equal to).

Note that these are the same options we used when setting criteria in Query Design.

If more than one of the conditions is *True*, only the code statements enclosed by the first true condition are executed. Normally you want to organize your *If...Then* statement so that the most likely alternative is evaluated first.

```
If condition Then
[statements]
End If
```

For example:

```
If intCPUTemp > 125 Then
    MsgBox "CPU is Overheating!"
End If
```

This example compares the value of an integer, intCPUTemp, to 125. If it exceeds 125, a message box displays the overheating message. If the value of intCPUTemp does not exceed 125, the part of the instruction after *Then* is ignored and the message box is not displayed.

Evaluating Multiple Cases

If you have a number of conditions to check besides just one, you can use the *Do...Case* statement. This allows you to evaluate a number of different options and then do nothing or, again, if all of the options are *False*, you can have an Otherwise clause that runs code, or simply do nothing.

One option for the *Do...Case* option is *Select Case*. It is like *If...Then* except you can choose from more than two alternatives. For example, we have a string variable called *strUserName*. It then gives privileges based on the results.

```
Select Case strUserName
    Case "Administrator"
        [Give the user Administrator privileges]
    Case "User"
        [Give the user User-Level privileges]
    Case Else
        [Give the user guest-level privileges]
End Select
```

The *Select Case* structure is ideal for testing the value of an expression against ranges of possible values. This example shows how to use the *Select Case* structure to evaluate a number against four different ranges and determine a bonus based on an individual range of values.

```
Select Case intTestNumber    'Test expression
    Case 1                   'If equal to 1
        Bonus = 0           'Bonus is 0
    Case 2, 3               'If either 2 or 3
        Bonus = .05         'Bonus is 5%
    Case 4 To 6             'If between 4 and 6
        Bonus = .10         'Bonus is 10%
    Case Else               'If anything else
        Bonus = .2          'Bonus is 20%
End Select
```

Note that we can add comments to our code by using the apostrophe. Anything after the apostrophe is not processed as part of the code. This allows us to explain the code and thus is an important part of the coding process.

Looping

Finally, there are the loop commands. They allow you run through a set of conditions until complete. You could say that this expands the *Do... Case* functionality to an unlimited number of options. Normally you run a loop through a data set but can be other uses. There are two basic options for looping:

1. *Do...Loop*
2. *For...Next*

For the *Do...Loop* approach, you can evaluate an expression at the beginning of the loop or at the end. *Do While...Loop* tests the expression and if *True*, repeats the code until the test expression evaluates as *False*. *Do Until...Loop* tests the expression and if *False*, repeats the code until the test expression evaluates as *True*.

This example tests for the EndOfFile condition and reads lines until the end of the file is reached:

```
Do While EndOfFile = False
    [Read and process next record in file]
    [Set EndOfFile to True if end of file is encountered]
    Exit Do
Loop
```

Chapter Review

You learned how to tie together your application using macros or VBA. We also discussed the difference between using macros and Visual Basic for Applications (VBA). Finally, we covered VBA by giving more detail about Event-driven programming, the approach VBA uses.

Lab

Continuing with the Training Management System, try to create a module with a function procedure for opening the forms you created in the previous lab. Try applying your procedure to the Buttons on your switchboard form.

Chapter 8
Implement

Chapter Overview

This chapter examines Part 7 of the Blueprint; implement your database. It provides information needed to make a database application available for other people to use. We will cover procedures for testing and setting up an application, as well as database administrator functions such as backing up data, security, and maintenance.

Goals for Learning

- Learn how to roll out your database application.
- Understand the need to test the application.
- Understand the functions of the DBA.

Questions to Answer as You Read

1. What do you need to do to roll out your database application?
2. What goes into testing the application?
3. What are the functions of the DBA?

Terms to Know

DBA
ODBC
Roll out

Implement

(NOTE: *Roll out* and *DBA* are also defined earlier in the book)

Roll Out the Application

You need to give thought to how you **roll out** your database application so that people can actually use it.

> To roll out your database application means to install the final version so that everyone actually uses it to do their database work instead of whatever other method they were using. As part of the Roll out, you normally include special publicity and training activities to prepare users for this action.

Testing could be said to be part of the roll out process. You want to make sure that what you build for users actually works. You test by gathering people who try to "break" the system. In other words, they do all of the activities that users need to do on the database application and then try things that users probably wouldn't do to make sure the application holds up. You carry out testing by gathering the right people to help. This could include personnel from one department. Also, you should designate one or two (or more depending on how large the application is) people from the Information Systems department to test.

You also want a system for tracking errors and fixes, which you will continue to follow even after you roll out the database application. This is version control, where you make sure your users always have the current version of the application. However, you also must make sure that when you install a new version that you back up the actual data so that the new data is not overwritten. This is particularly important if the changes needed require table design changes versus just changes to the user interface or reports.

Part of testing and change management is to identify power users in each department who can serve as *champions* of the new system. You can get them involved in testing as well and then when they see the benefits, they can communicate the advantages of the new system to others.

Part of the roll out effort also involves training. As a business leader, you want to make sure users understand how to do their work with the new database application. As mentioned before, this is part of change management. So, in the training, you don't just want to *talk about* the new database application. You still need to continue to *sell* users on the new system and how it will benefit them so that the transition to the new system will be as smooth as possible. For this reason, make sure the training focuses on the actual business activities the users need to know versus just explaining features of the new database application. Also, keep reminding the users how this new system will save them time and make their work easier. If the new database application makes work for users harder and longer versus easier, then one wonders why the new system was adopted (see earlier sections of the book!). Ideally, training materials should be developed earlier than later. In other words, business leaders should go back and look at the specifications for the database application and make sure roll out training answers the questions and meets the requests of the earlier specifications. You want to make sure that the training meets user expectations as much as possible.

Training should be *just-in-time*. In other words, you should time training so that users receive it as they will start using the new database application. Training that comes too soon will be forgotten or not a priority for users since they don't need to know it immediately. Another option is to set up a test site that is not the live data. Then users can actually enter information and generate reports as part of the training. But, again, they should be able to access the live data as soon as possible after the training.

Finally, training should include documentation materials that remind users of how to complete certain business functions with the database application. You would basically be writing a procedure for doing work which includes interactions with the database.

Assign a Database Administrator

It is essential to assign someone the role of Database Administrator (**DBA**) for the on-going use of the database application.

> *The Database Administrator is the person responsible for identifying and taking care of all the data in the organization.*

In larger companies, this may be an entire department. In smaller companies or organizations, it may be another function that someone takes on. The main thing is that as a business leader, you are aware of the need to have this role filled. Let's talk in more detail about some of the responsibilities of the DBA.

We mentioned the DBA function earlier in the book; that they are like *data accountants*. So, one responsibility of the DBA is to make sure there is enough storage room for data, make sure the data is good, make sure the data is regularly backed up, and at times run checks for possible anomalies (errors or even unethical activity) in the data. As you can see, the DBA needs to interact with different groups in the organization; the network administrator (regarding traffic caused by use of the database), hardware (regarding storage space on site or elsewhere), and even users who need to know what fields they might need from what tables to build reports.

The DBA also creates and maintains the data dictionary (mentioned earlier in the book). Organizations can become overwhelmed and confused with different sets of data and lose track of how much redundancy (having basically the same field and resulting data in different tables) there is in their various databases. Decisions for new database applications should include a plan for how the new system fits in with the current data dictionary. If the new system (and data design) is going to replace an old system, then the DBA should be *front and center* in managing the moving of the old data into the new system.

As mentioned, the DBA is responsible for backing up data. Normally backups can be automated. However, the DBA should periodically check the backup data to make sure it is good. Also, there should be a backup plan in place which includes current backups and older backups that are stored and then removed over time. Also, backups should take place in two locations; one on site (or easily accessible) and one offsite. But, be careful about the selection of an offsite storage option as data security is paramount.

The DBA oversees data security, again most likely in conjunction with the network administrator. Roles and/or groups should be defined with specific permissions granted. For larger companies, consideration might be given to granting read-only access to data in the ERP that can be accessed through, for example, an Access **ODBC** connection.

Open Database Connectivity (ODBC) is a Microsoft interface for accessing data from a variety of DBMSs.

Then the data can be used in new and smaller departmental-level database applications. But, again, care must be given as to what data can be available through an ODBC connection. The trade-off, as always, is between security and functionality. This is why business ethics is important in organizations. Ethical personnel will respect data and use it correctly. So, ethical organizations have more opportunities for efficiency gains through departmental-level applications.

As far as Access goes, it does have security. However, it is better to use other security options (perhaps in conjunction with Access security). For example, if you are using Access to link to, for example, SQL Server data then you can set security levels (at least for the data) on the SQL Server side which will be in place when attached to Access via an ODBC connection. You can also constrain access to an Access database through network security. You can put the data for the Access application on a network drive that is controlled by network security to determine who can access it and who can make changes to it.

Finally, the DBA needs to *tune* the data. This can be a complex set of tasks but at a fundamental level, it means rebuilding indexes or using the **Access Database Tools** menu option called **Compact and Repair Database**. As data is added and deleted and objects changes, space can be made which can slow things down. Using the utility basically *cleans up* the space and makes the database work as efficiently as possible.

Chapter Review

This chapter explored how to roll out your database. We also covered procedures for testing and setting up an application, as well as database administrator functions such as backing up the data, security, and maintenance.

Lab

Make a plan for rolling out a database application. Make sure to assign someone to the role of DBA and write out responsibilities.

Conclusion

Thank you for taking time to read this book. As a business leader, you are the one who will benefit your organization by understanding and implementing some of the principles discussed. You also may find that you can actually do some of the database work on your own. But at minimum, you will be much better informed when working with others who are doing the implementation. In any case, you will make a positive difference!

Glossary

Action query	An action query makes changes to the requested data and does not display it.
Analytics	Using internal and external data in tradition and non-traditional formats to develop and test hypotheses for solving business problems.
Application flow	How the user interface (mainly forms) leads the user to the different features of the entire application in order to accomplish required business tasks.
Archiving	Archiving is the process of extracting and storing historical business data which is no longer required for current activity but maintained for decision support and analytics.
Assumptions	Assumptions are events that you believe must happen if your project will finish on schedule.
Attaching	Attaching means to use outside data with your database so that there is only one copy, the original.

Blueprint	A blueprint is an overall plan of design.
Bottom Up approach to data design	Starting with no basic data design of tables, you simply list all the fields that you will need, organize the fields (that represent a similar group, thing, or activity), and then create the tables that you need to contain the fields.
Bound control	A control on a form or report that shows values from a field.
Business process	Business processes are the activities which occur on a regular basis in an organization to carry out its operations.
Business rules	Business rules are written (or understood) guidelines of what happens in a company. For example, a business rule for invoice payment might read: *We pay all invoices that are two weeks old or older on the last Friday of the month.*
Calculated fields	Calculated fields are fields created in queries which do not appear in any database table. They are used to display data calculated from other table fields and, like a regular field, can accept record selection criteria.
Candidate key	A Candidate key is a field or fields in a table that uniquely identifies each record but is not necessarily the primary key.

Cascade delete	When Referential Integrity is enforced, if a record is deleted in the main table, all of the records in the linked table with the same key value will also be deleted.
Cascade update	When Referential Integrity is enforced, if the value of the Primary key is changed in the main table, all of the values of the Foreign key fields in the linked table will be updated with that same value.
CASE	CASE (Computer Aided Software Engineering) uses software to model business activities and then translates into database application objects, primarily tables.
Change order	A change order is a document that describes work that you will do that adds to the original scope of the project and allows you to charge for these additional hours.
Class module	A Class module contains procedures that run in response to certain events associated with the object; a form or report.
Client	The client is the person or persons who ask you do the work and sign off on the work.

Client-server database	A larger DBMS that puts the data on a server (locally or "in the cloud"), called the "server" or "back-end," and puts everything else in a separate place, usually on the user machine, called the "client" or "front-end,"
Code	The code (or lines of code) is the individual lines of instruction that make up a procedure or a program. It is like a sentence (code) in an entire book (the program). These may also be called statements.
Column	A Column (also called a Field) is a place to store a particular detail that you want to know about a group, thing, or activity (table).
Command	Specific options under a Menu. For example, in Microsoft Word, the Commands under the File menu include: New...; Open...; Close (NOTE: In Microsoft Access, you can also run commands by using macros or VBA.
Composite key	A Composite key field is a combination of two or more fields that together are unique.
Contingency	A contingency is something unknown that will happen to increase the time required to finish the work.

Contrived key	A Contrived key is a field that is created specifically as a unique identifier and does not represent any actual information in the business.
Controls	Controls are tools for form and report objects that allow you to show data, text or links to websites, graphics, or other files.
Data	A representation of business activity.
Data clean-up	Data clean-up involves making sure data is in normal form (mainly removing duplicate data) before using. This is accomplished by using queries.
Data design	Data design is the of process of deciding which tables you need and which fields you need in those tables to accurately represent the people, things and activities in your real organization and how those people and activities relate to each other.
Data Dictionary	A "database of the data" and includes all organizational databases and all tables and fields included in those databases.
Data flow diagram	A diagram of how data flows through a database application.
Data management	Your approach for keeping track of your business activities.
Data Sources	The tables and fields (from those tables) used as input to a query.

Database Administrator (DBA)	The Database Administrator is the person responsible for identifying and taking care of all the data in the organization.
Database application	Uses the special features of a DBMS like Microsoft Access to build an easy-to-use, menu-driven system for users.
Database Development Perspective	The Database Development perspective describes the database features that you will build to accomplish the work objective.
Database Development standard	A Database Development standard is an agreed-upon way of doing your work.
Database management	Using an electronic way to store and then use your business data.
Database Management System (DBMS)	The specific software package that you use for data management; like Microsoft Access.
Database platform	The database platform is the Operating System, the computer and network, the database software on which the data is kept and stored.
Date type mismatch	Error (usually in a query or when entering data) that occurs when the data that you want to work with is a different data type than the data type that the field requires.
Decision makers	The decision makers are the people who approve your work and ultimately benefit from your work.

Decision Support Systems	Decision Support Systems use your DBMS to pull data from many different places to help you make decisions
Declaring a variable	Declaring a variable is when you name the variable and give it a type (such as Text or Numeric or Form) at the beginning of a procedure or as part of the name of the procedure.
Developers	Developers create database applications that users can work with.
Documentation	Documentation is a written explanation of what you did.
Duration	Duration is the amount of calendar time you take to complete that task.
Dynaset	Temporary virtual tables created by execution of a query. A new dynaset is created for each execution of a query and only includes records and fields selected in that particular query. Dynasets are available for use by other database objects.
Enterprise Resource Planning System	Enterprise Resource Planning (ERP) systems are database applications used by large companies to manage all of their daily activities.
Entity	An entity is simply some aspect of the organization that is necessary to accomplish work like a person, activity or thing.

Entity-Relationship Diagram	An Entity-Relationship Diagram shows the items in the organization, how they relate to one another, and perhaps how this activity in the organization translates into data design.
Error checking	Writing code to check potential errors that might occur and provide a user-friendly way to work out the problem. Error checking can also be called error trapping.
Event	An event is something that the user does while using your application. Your routine will respond to this event and run.
Event procedure	An event procedure is a particular procedure that runs in response to a certain event attached to an object in a form or report.
Event-driven programming	Event-driven programming creates code to react to the actions (called *events*) that the user takes.
Expression	A combination of values, operators, functions and object identifiers which are put together to find a result you are looking for.
Expression Builder	Tool for building criteria for query record selection and query processing.
Field	A field (also called a column) is a place to store a particular detail that you want to know about a group, thing, or activity (table).

Fixed price bid	A fixed-price bid is a bid where you give one price for all the work that you do on a project. You must stick to the original bid for time and cost.
Foreign key (FK)	A Foreign key is a field in one table that is a primary key in a different table and allows you to link tables together in order to share information.
Function	A function is a series of instructions (normally calculations) carried out all at once. It is more efficient than carrying out each step separately. You can also pass information (called parameters) that the function uses as part of its calculation.
Function procedure	A Function is a procedure that does accept variables. It also can refer to the results of calculation that returns a value.
Functional Dependency	A Functional Dependency is a relationship between (usually) two fields where the value of one depends on the other.
Importing	Importing means to bring outside data into your database so that there are two copies, the original and the copy that is now in your database.
Index	An index is a special file stored in the database that increases performance.

Information Systems (IS) group	The Information Systems (IS) group OR Information Technology (IT) group is the organizational group that supports technology hardware and software and infrastructure, including database administration.
Inner-join	Type of join where the only records that are included from either table are the ones that have a common field value.
Join	The act of actually connecting two common fields together from two different tables. This is the means by which the relationship takes place.
Key	The key fields establish relationships in data design.
Library	A library (called *module* in Access) is a group of programs in one place that you can use anywhere in the application; and can be stored in the same database or a different one.
Logical design	The technical name for the work definition part of specifications; one of the two perspectives of laying out specifications,
Lookup table	A lookup table is a table that exists for data entry purposes. This limited number of options is also called a domain or range of options.
Loop	A loop is a code technique that goes through a number of checks until a condition is met.

Macro	A macro is taking several (micro) steps that you would normally do manually and running them all at once.
Main database objects	Main database objects in Access are the ones that are listed on the tabs on the main Database Window of Access.
Management Information Systems	Management Information Systems work with Transaction Processing database applications to help manage and carry out business data activities for you.
Menu	An option on a Menu bar. For example, in Microsoft Word, the Menus on the main Menu bar include: File, Edit, View.
Menu bar	A Menu bar is a bar at the top of the screen (normally above any toolbars) that includes the particular menus that are available.
Method	Methods are actions that you can take with on an object or actions that the object can do. It is like a procedure that has already been written as part of VBA.
Milestone	A milestone is a distinctive task of zero duration that indicates an important accomplishment in the project.

Module	A module (also called *library*) is a collection of procedures in one place which makes it easier to manage. You might say that a module is a library that contains a group of procedures.
Multi-Valued Dependency	A Multi-Valued Dependency is a situation where for every value of one field, you can have multiple values of a different field.
Natural key	A Natural key is a field that is used as a Primary key field in a table and represents some characteristic that is present in organization.
Normalization	Setting up tables and the fields in those tables so that they follow certain rules that prevent errors (particularly duplicate information) in the data that you will store. These rules are called "normal form."
Object	An object is simply something that you work with when doing database development; like a table, field, query, form or report.
Object description	An Object description in the Access database world is a particular property for an object where you can simply explain what the thing is and does.

Object event	An object event is simply one of the events that is available for a certain object (usually on a form). For example, a combo box control has certain events associated with it. A check box control has different events associated with it. The entire form object has a different set of events.
Open Database Connectivity (ODBC)	A Microsoft interface for accessing data from a variety of DBMSs.
Outer-join	Type of join where all the records from one table are included and the records from the other table that have a common field value with the first table are also included.
Output	To output your data means to show certain pieces of the data in a certain format on the computer screen or on a piece of paper from the printer. The output shows you answers to questions from the data.
Parameter	A value that gives input to a function. The value is entered or pulled from another object when the function is run.
PERT	PERT (Program Evaluation and Review Technique) is a visual way of showing how different tasks relate to one another.

Phase	A phase is a development project that meets customer desires for productivity but does not necessarily satisfy all of their desires.
Physical design	The technical name for the database definition part of specifications; one of the two perspectives of laying out specifications.
Power user	A Power user can use data to answer questions. Tables, queries and reporting OR "Power users know how to work from the Access Database Window to find answers to questions and report the results."
Primary key (PK)	A Primary key is a field (or fields) that uniquely identify each record.
Procedure	A procedure (also called a *program*) is a specific set of code that accomplishes some task or calculates a value. It is a small program that has a distinct focus. Procedures are common in Event-driven programming. A procedure can also be called a *routine*.
Process diagram	A diagram of business process; how work flows across functional areas to deliver a product or service to a customer.
Program	A computer program is a set of individual instructions that tell the computer what to do.

Programming	Programming is the process of writing the code that will run and carry out instructions.
Programming Language	A programming language is a form of communication that gives instructions to the computer to take specific actions. Just like we have many different spoken languages, we have different programming languages.
Programs	A computer program is a set of individual instructions that tell the computer what to do.
Project management	Project management is the process of planning, describing, and tracking a job so that the work is completed on time and close to the budget.
Property	Some characteristic that you can change about an object.
Proposal	The proposal is simply the document that you create that details what you discovered in the previous two steps: *Talk with Your Team* and *Work Out the Database Features*.
Prototype	A prototype is a working example presented to the client for feedback.
Query	A query is a question asked about data contained in the database tables or action that needs to be taken. Queries are created and can be stored as database objects.

Query Design Grid	The Query Design Grid is a fully featured query development tool in Microsoft Access that allows you to create queries using multiple tables and/or other queries and provides the ability to set criteria and query type.
Record	A Record (also called *Row*) is the actual business data entered in a group of fields in a table … like a file folder.
Record locking	Record locking follows rules to make sure that only one person is changing the record at a time and that others who are trying to change know this. Record locking maintains the integrity of the data in a fair way.
Record selection	The process of including or excluding records from a query dynaset. Record selection criteria are user defined.
Referential Integrity	Referential Integrity means that when you have a relationship between two tables, you are linking the proper record(s) together; each and every record in one table matches the proper record in the other table.
Relationship	A Relationship is a link that you make between tables based on a common field that allows you to use data from both tables in your outputs.

Ribbon	The horizontal bar that normally appears at the top of a Window where your main menu choices appear. When you click on a menu choice from the menu bar, a vertical list of options appears.
Roll out	To roll out your database application means to install the final version so that everyone actually uses it to do their database work instead of whatever other method they were using. As part of the Roll out, you normally include special publicity and training activities to prepare users for this action.
Rollback	When changing several pieces of data; if all the changes do not take place as planned, all of the changes are undone and reset to their original values, thus protecting the integrity of the data.
Running the program	The program runs when it carries out the instructions found on each line of code. In event-driven programming, it runs in response to a certain event.
Scope	Scope is describing exactly what you will produce or perform in the project and what you will not produce or perform.
Sections	Sections add data and organization to Access Reports or Forms including grouping, subtotals, and grand totals.

Select query	A Select (sometimes classified as *Show*) query simply retrieves the requested data in the format and order requested and displays it.
Specification	A specification is a visual and/or written statement that describes what work your database will do for the people in your organization and the database features you will build to accomplish this work objective.
SQL (Structured Query Language)	The accepted standard for writing queries. Syntax may vary slightly depending on the DBMS you use.
Standard module	A Standard module contains procedures that are not associated with any particular object and can be run anywhere within your database.
Storyboard	A set of graphics in order to represent "scenes" in a movie, for example, or layout steps in database applications or websites.
Sub procedure	A Sub is a procedure that completes some task and does not accept variables.
Subform	A subform is a form that appears within a form, linked by a common field (or field); normally showing a one-to-many relationship in one place.
Successful applications	A successful application, is one that is useful to the organization, done in a timely way, and that people actually use.

Switchboard	A switchboard (or navigation form) is like a menu on a form. It provides buttons that the user will push to take them to different parts of the database.
System table	A System table is a table that contains information that you use in your database application.
Tab Order	When you are using a form (Form view) in Access, the Tab Order determines where the cursor moves when you press the Tab key.
Table	A table represents a particular group, thing or activity in the organization that you want to know about.
Task	A task is one specific piece of work that you do to help you complete your job.
Technical Support personnel	Technical Support personnel are the people from the IS group who will install your database on the network and make sure the right people can access it.
Top Down approach to data design	Starting with a basic data design of tables and fields that fits a general business function and then adjusting the design to meet the particular requirements of the customer.
Transaction Processing Systems	Transaction Processing Systems are database applications that store, retrieve, and process data required for basic business activities.

Transitive Dependency	A Transitive Dependency is when the value of a field is determined by a field that is not the Primary key.
Unbound control	An Unbound control is a control that does not show data but can show calculations or other information like text.
User friendly	Normally refers to a database application or an aspect of the application and refers to how recognizable the different options are to the user making it easy to accomplish work.
User interface	A user interface is simply a user-friendly bridge between the organizational activities (real world) and the tables (data design or data world) and queries that reflect those activities. The bridge is normally the forms.
User interface design	The user interface design is the planned layout of forms to most efficiently and effectively guide users through the application.
Users	Users are people who use databases that other people create.
Validation	Setting up tables and fields and in some cases, using code in forms to check to make sure that the data entered is correct and disallowing an entry that is not correct.

Variable	A Variable is a temporary holder of information that needs a value that can change depending on the situation.
VBA	Visual Basic for Applications (VBA) is the programming language that comes with Microsoft Office products including Microsoft Access. It is a variation of Visual Basic and is useful because it is user friendly, yet powerful.
View	In Microsoft Access, this refers to different ways of looking at data or design (i.e. switching between Design View and Datasheet View). It can also refer to a particular subset of data that you are looking at.
Wizard	A Wizard is a development tool provided by Access for quickly creating query, form and report objects. Modifications cannot be made using the Wizard.
Work	Work is the actual time you spend on a task.
Work Accomplishment Perspective	The Work Accomplishment perspective describes what work your database will do for your organization.
Workgroup	A workgroup is a group of approximately two to thirty people who work in a specific task area in an organization.